Past
Lives
for Beginners

About the Author

Douglas De Long is a spiritual/personal counselor, past-life therapist, and chakra master. He has studied and developed his own psychic abilities and spiritual growth for over twenty-five years.

Born with the ability to see human auras, chakras, spirit guides, and angels, Douglas was always reading books about psychic and metaphysical subjects. But due to the nature of his stepfather's profession, he and his family traveled for many years and his psychic abilities started to close up from lack of use. It wasn't until after a near-death experience at the age of nineteen that he reawakened his childhood gifts.

Through numerous life lessons and years of metaphysical studies, Douglas was able to enhance his abilities and create a unique course that he has been teaching for more than fifteen years. In the past quarter century, he has regressed close to 1,500 individuals and students. He has been guided to put his knowledge and channeled teachings into book form in order to help people open up and develop their innate abilities.

Douglas De Long and his wife, Carol, reside in Saskatoon, Saskatchewan, where they own and operate the De Long Ancient Mystery School.

For more information, please visit www.douglasdelong.com.

Past
Lives

For Beginners

A Guide to Reincarnation & Techniques
to Improve Your Present Life

Douglas De Long

Llewellyn Publications
Woodbury, Minnesota

FIRST EDITION
First Printing, 2013

Cover design by Adrienne Zimiga
Cover images: Woman on left: Joyce Vincent/Shutterstock.com
              Woman on right: iStockphoto.com/Iconogenic
              Black clock face: pjmorley/Shutterstock.com
              White clock face: Meder Lorant/Shutterstock.com
Interior illustrations by Llewellyn Art Department

Llewellyn Publications is a registered trademark of Llewellyn Worldwide Ltd.

Library of Congress Cataloging-in-Publication Data
De Long, Douglas, 1954–
   Past lives for beginners : a guide to reincarnation & techniques to improve your present life / Douglas De Long. — First Edition.
      pages   cm
   Includes bibliographical references.
   ISBN 978-0-7387-3517-7
   1. Reincarnation. I. Title.
   BP573.R5D4 2013
   133.901'35—dc23
                              2012050874

Llewellyn Worldwide Ltd. does not participate in, endorse, or have any authority or responsibility concerning private business transactions between our authors and the public.

All mail addressed to the author is forwarded, but the publisher cannot, unless specifically instructed by the author, give out an address or phone number.

Any Internet references contained in this work are current at publication time, but the publisher cannot guarantee that a specific location will continue to be maintained. Please refer to the publisher's website for links to authors' websites and other sources.

Cover models used for illustrative purposes only and may not endorse or represent the book's subject.

Llewellyn Publications
A Division of Llewellyn Worldwide Ltd.
2143 Woodale Drive
Woodbury, MN 55125-2989
www.llewellyn.com

Printed in the United States of America

contents

introduction

For more than twenty-five years, I have been a past-life therapist. I have regressed more than a thousand individuals during that time. Through it all I have met many unique characters who have explored their respective past lives and blessed me with the opportunity to help each of them on their own spiritual journeys.

My wife, Carol, and I founded the De Long Ancient Mystery School in Saskatoon, Canada, almost fifteen years ago. It was our intention then, as it still is now, to help others awaken their true psychic and spiritual potential within. We teach psychic development classes and ancient healing techniques, and provide spiritual counseling and energy healing for people in the area. Past-life therapy has always been one of the many services that is provided through our unique school. People have come from far and wide to take our classes and to explore their past lives through therapy.

I have used my reputation as an international author to promote our school along with the services that we provide. We have traveled throughout Canada and the United States in order to reach and teach people seeking to explore their gifts and enhance their spirituality. Reincarnation has always been one of the most fascinating subjects that many of our students and clients show intense interest in. Exploring a previous lifetime is one of the most powerful tools that can be used by someone to understand their true self.

Between radio and television interviews, book signings, article writing, and teaching classes, I have been able to work at what I love to do. I strongly believe that I am following my path, my life purpose. At our mystery school, we continue to help others on their spiritual journeys.

I live in a medium-sized city in Western Canada. Many of the people living here neither embrace nor explore their spirituality. In fact, as a past-life therapist living here, many of the residents I meet feel uncomfortable with the type of work that I do. For many people, reincarnation is a subject that they do not believe in. Others may believe in reincarnation but do not wish to pursue this fascinating phenomenon. This attitude shown toward my work only stiffens my resolve to follow the path I am on. The more people

I can help to explore their own past lives, the better I feel about what I do and what I strongly believe in.

It is my hope and intention to help you recall many of your past lives. At the same time, I want to assist you in developing your potential psychic and spiritual gifts. These gifts allow you to access even more information about your previous embodiments on Earth. When you explore a past life, you can heal the past, change the present, and affect your future in a more positive way. Our traits, our characteristics, our idiosyncrasies, and our unexplained physical as well as emotional pains can sometimes be traced back to previous incarnations. Some of our gifts that we have are brought forward from the past. For instance, the 14th Dalai Lama, Tenzin Gyatzo, both the head of state and spiritual leader of Tibet, most likely came back into a physical body with the knowledge and information he had from a previous lifetime.

As a child, I would often see visions or memories from some of my past lives. I would be fascinated by certain time periods and regions of the world. For instance, watching movies about ancient Egypt and reading anything that I could in regard to this wondrous civilization became a mild obsession on my part. In my mind, I could envision the scenery of that area, including the mighty Nile with palms trees blowing gently in the warm breeze. Even the smell of exotic flowers and others scents from that ancient land would be very real to me in this lifetime. It is this fascination with my previous lifetimes that has influenced me greatly and placed me onto the special path that I follow. It encourages me to guide others to explore their own past lives as well.

Although this book is a teaching instrument, it is also much more than that. Along with several exercises and techniques designed to help you recall many of your past lives, funny, informative, and inspirational case studies are shared with you too. From these stories and case studies within the pages of *Past Lives for Beginners*, you will see the great potential of past-life recall and recognize the true value of reincarnation. Please be aware that all of the names mentioned in this book have been changed in order to protect the confidentiality of my clients.

As you explore your own past lives, you will discover numerous things about yourself. You will recognize that you are the culmination of many previous lifetimes. Soon, you will develop or enhance more of your spiritual gifts and psychic abilities. You will know that you are truly eternal and that you are loved and protected by angelic beings and spirit guides. These beings of light can assist you when you explore your past lives. As you recall past lives, you will start to astral travel more often. If you are already doing this, that is great! We will be discussing the close connection that exists between astral travel, reincarnation, and past-life regression later on.

All the techniques and exercises in the book will aid you to recall several of your previous embodiments upon this earth. I have successfully used these very same techniques personally and with clients for many years with great and productive results. Developing the ability to recall past lives involves more than just practicing meditation. It takes focus and direction with a clear intent to succeed.

When we are born, a veil closes down on most of us, hiding our memories of previous lives from us. In most cases, it takes special techniques to lift that heavy veil and gaze into the remote past. The techniques provided within the pages of this book will lift that veil, light the darkest recesses of your mind, and guide you to your past lives. Your higher self will assist in this process, allowing you to see and feel the past for your greatest spiritual growth.

If you can think of Planet Earth as a school where your soul learns and grows, you will then see this world in a very different light. You will recognize that schoolhouse Earth is a wondrous journey for your soul to embrace. All the trials, tribulations, joys, and events of life can be experienced, allowing your eternal soul to grow and blossom.

The mind and the soul are joined as one. Your mind as part of the immortal soul contains wisdom, knowledge, and memories from many past lives. You will be taught to tap into this great resource.

You will be taught all the techniques I employ in my past-life sessions with my clients. These techniques have been used for many years and work effectively. Roughly 85 percent of the people I have worked with over the last twenty-five years have had great success with the implementation of these exercises and unique techniques.

From years of experience and research, I know that one out of every three people can be hypnotized in the traditional way. Many of my clients and students have mentioned to me that they cannot be hypnotized. A few of the techniques I employ are designed to work with your chakras, or energy centers. By using the chakras, you can feel this energy flow throughout your body. This also slows down the brain-wave patterns and allows you to drift. Most people will feel very relaxed and allow themselves to enter into the deep state of consciousness that is necessary to receive past-life information. People who have a more difficult time being hypnotized find that moving energy through the body lets them enter into a hypnotic state without the use of hypnotism.

The chakra-energy techniques explained in this book are very effective and will help you to experience your own past lives.

Many people experience past-life recall from hundreds or even thousands of years ago. Some people will remember an ancient lifetime. These types of past-life experiences cannot be verified with documents such as birth certificates, family photographs, marriage licenses, death certificates, and other printed matter.

However, some people will recall past lives that happened in the relatively recent past. When this happens, these individuals can do their own research. A client of mine, Roger, is a great example of someone who successfully researched his own information about his last lifetime. Although he was very aware of its manifold horrors, Roger had always held a fascination with Nazi Germany. He collected Nazi memorabilia, including some books containing photographs. His initial regression work with me only added to his interest in exploring that lifetime, since it explained the lifelong interest he'd had in his present life.

At one point, Roger showed me a particular book that contained several photographs that were pertinent to his previous embodiment. He flipped through the book until he found a photograph of an airfield in Germany. In it were several World War II German planes. With excitement he pointed to the page and said, "See the man standing beside the plane near the back of the field? That's me!" And indeed we did confirm that it was an officer in the Luftwaffe, the air force of Nazi Germany, who had been revealed to him in a past-life experience, in which he died in a fiery plane crash around 1943. Roger mentioned his rank, his name, and a great deal of intimate detail about that lifetime as he talked to me.

Roger continued turning the pages of the book and found another photograph. He pointed to a photograph of Adolf Hitler and several of his military staff who were at a function in a huge ballroom. Obviously, the photographer had taken the picture from the other side of the room. His eyes held a gleam as he stated, "I remember standing right beside the photographer when he took the picture. I had just been given a medal for bravery." When it's possible, this kind of research can be very rewarding with its confirmation.

The Many Reasons for Past-Life Regression

Over the years I have had the same question presented to me in different ways. My own mother, may she rest in peace, voiced this very question: "Douglas, my life has been very hard. It has been hell at times. Why would I want to know about another past life?" Fair enough. This is an honest and valid question.

At that time I did not have an answer for her or, for that matter, anyone else who voiced this insightful question. It took some deep soul-searching followed by years of working as a past-life therapist and spiritual counselor to receive the right answer. For many of you, the answer is very simple.

When you look at a past life, you can heal from it, change the present in a positive manner, and ultimately create a better future for yourself. In other words, if you can heal the past, you can also heal your present lifetime and the immediate future. The veil that comes down on you during the traumatic process of being born, causing you to forget your past incarnations, can be lifted through past-life regression. There are many reasons to delve into the past, exploring your previous lives:

- **Emotional healing.** Anger, sadness, grief, hatred, and other negative emotions created by past-life events can be brought up to the surface of your conscious mind and be released safely. A permanent healing can then occur.
- **Physical healing.** Unexplained pains and health issues that plague you, and which cannot be healed through conventional medicine, can be traced in many cases to previous incarnations. By "re-living" the accident or death scene, you can bring the memory of the pain to the consciousness of your mind

and thereby release the pain. A profound healing of long-standing problems may then take place.

- **Releasing of fears and phobias.** Unexplained fears and unfounded phobias can be remembered through past-life recall, brought to the surface of the conscious mind, analyzed, and released quickly. Soon a fear or phobia that hounded you for many years will no longer exist, or at least not affect you as much.
- **Understanding and healing of relationship problems.** The recall of a past-life relationship with someone who you are involved with now will help you to recognize negative patterns in the relationship, allowing you to break or heal these patterns. You will understand where love-hate relationships originate.
- **Receiving of gifts and attributes.** By exploring a past life, you will not only recall that incarnation but also in some situations remember or relearn certain gifts and attributes. For example, if you were a healer using herbs in an earlier lifetime, you will be able to reawaken some of your knowledge of herbs. This is a form of super learning.

A past-life experience can be achieved through guided meditation, astral travel, hypnotherapy, or through past-life recall either with the help of an experienced professional or on your own. Any or all of these options can be great tools to truly explore your soul's journey.

Through either a guided meditation or a deep meditation you do yourself, you can slow down your brainwave patterns, open up your subconscious mind, and start to recall past lives. Breathing and meditation techniques will be explained within the pages of this book in order to help you enter the right altered state of consciousness. This state will allow you to start accessing past-life information. You have the potential within to explore your own previous incarnations. This will open up many doors on a spiritual level for you.

Throughout this book, you will be presented with detailed exercises and techniques designed to help you recall some of your past lives. Many of these techniques will also help you to awaken or enhance your psychic and spiritual gifts.

As a human being, you are multidimensional. Your soul can exist here on the earthly plane now yet be able to remember many previous lifetimes. As an eternal soul, you have traveled back and forth between Heaven and Earth many times. The techniques within *Past Lives for Beginners*, along with the case studies, will help you to recognize your soul within and embrace your full potential. Enjoy your spiritual journey that you are about to embark upon!

one

All About Reincarnation

I believe that it is essential to appreciate our potential as human beings and recognize the importance of inner transformation.
—THE DALAI LAMA

To be born into a physical body, to live and die, and then to be reborn into another physical form: this is the central concept of reincarnation or past-life belief. The belief in this process of transforming is fast becoming a part of the culture of Western society as more people awaken within themselves. The theory of reincarnation has been accepted in Eastern society for thousands of years; in fact, it forms the core belief in Hinduism and Buddhism. This is one of the reasons why many people in Western countries are now embracing Buddhism.

Reincarnation—the belief that you have lived before—answers many questions that pertain to your reason for being here on Earth. It helps put your life into proper perspective and gives you a better understanding of the cycle of life and death.

Many believe we have an eternal soul that enters the physical body at the time of birth, and that the soul resides in this material form during a lifetime. At the moment of death, that very soul, your soul, then leaves the body (the shell) and journeys back to Heaven. If you accept this concept readily, why not the concept of reincarnation? After all, if the immortal soul can come down to Earth and join with a physical body once, why not a second time?

Some people think that once you are dead, you are dead. As far as they are concerned, your body rots in the ground and there is nothing afterwards. You become a meal for the earthworms and fertilizer for the soil. I feel that to believe that you are here only for a few short years and pass into oblivion or nothingness at the end of that lifetime is a very sad way of looking at the wonders of living. This attitude toward life hinders the soul growth of that person. When a person has this attitude, the soul is held back slightly and is not allowed to grow. This belief puts up a slight block and interferes with the enlightenment of the human soul.

Ironically, the soul will end up returning to Earth for another learning lesson—a lesson, one hopes, that teaches the person that the human soul is immortal and of value.

When you become more awakened and follow a spiritual path, you will be aware of your own immortality.

In the days of Jesus, reincarnation was considered common knowledge; it was accepted as part of life. The original teachings of Jesus also involved the theory of reincarnation. Unfortunately, many of these references to reincarnation by Jesus and other great spiritual teachers were carefully deleted from ancient texts that were considered part of the Bible. (It is believed that Emperor Constantine, during the Council of Nicaea in 325 CE, wanted any references to reincarnation removed from the Bible. No one knows for sure exactly what happened, but the ultimate goal was to have control of the population. As a result, many books were removed and never made it into the current Bible.)

In her groundbreaking book, *Reincarnation: The Missing Link in Christianity*, author Elizabeth Clare Prophet makes the case that Jesus taught reincarnation. The author traces the history of reincarnation in Christianity—from Jesus and the early Christians through Church councils and the persecution of so-called heretics.

In 1945, near Nag Hammadi, Egypt, a collection of ancient books was discovered. These books are known as the Gnostic Gospels. These included the Secret Gospel of Thomas, the Gospel of Philip, and the Gospel of Mary, which contained the words of Mary Magdalene. *Gnosis,* or the knowledge of God, was taught within these ancient writings, writings that held a different philosophy than the books that were eventually approved as books of the Bible. Hence, all of these ancient texts were removed.

Most of the bishops and leaders of the early but rapidly growing Christian Church removed several books from this sacred literature, including these writings, in the hopes of removing any and all references to reincarnation (at the Council of Nicaea). These men were striving for power, and they wanted to control the population and ultimately the known world of the time (i.e., the Roman Empire). By eliminating the idea of birth to rebirth from their doctrine, replacing it instead with the idea of only one lifetime per person followed by either eternal hell or Heaven depending on the person's actions, their belief created a greater need for the Christian Church as a salvation from death.

This concept of Heaven and hell has been lessening its grip on people as they seek a more spiritual path, discovering on their journey the real teachings of Jesus and the teachings of the mystery schools that existed back then. Jesus taught healing techniques that involved the laying on of hands, reincarnation, the removal of negative energy from the human soul, and much more.

Despite the early Church's attempt at censoring, there are some specific references to reincarnation still found within the pages of the present Bible. In the New Testament, in the Book of Matthew, an intimation is made to John the Baptist as the returning prophet, Elias:

> *For all the prophets and the law have prophesied until John.*
>
> *And if you are willing to receive it, he is Elias who has come.*

Matthew 11:13–14

A similar intimation is also mentioned again in Matthew 17:10–13.

The Nature of Reincarnation

Mystical wisdom and esoterically hidden messages were described as they appear within the Bible. The mention of the Holy Ghost or Holy Spirit itself in the Bible has a connection to the theory of reincarnation. Let us discuss this. When early Christianity borrowed the doctrine of the Holy Trinity from teachings derived from ancient Hinduism, it also created a hidden, mystical message in this idea.

The ancient mystery schools and healing temples taught the concept of reincarnation under what was called the Law of the Triangle or the Law of Three. They taught this belief for hundreds of years. Jesus also taught this to his many disciples, both male and female, during his lifetime.

In his book *The Secret Doctrines of Jesus*, H. Spencer Lewis, the late imperator of the Rosicrucians, refers to this:

> *That among the one hundred and twenty members were not only those who were later known as the Twelve Disciples and who constituted the secret executive committee of this secret society, but also others who were interested in the mysterious, secret work of the society, including the mother of Jesus and his brothers and sisters.*

This Law of Three was a reference to the theory of reincarnation. The early Christian fathers—the more enlightened ones—blended the Holy Trinity of Hinduism with the Law of Three from the teachings of Jesus, creating the Holy

Trinity that Christianity now recognizes.[1] The Father, the Son, and the Holy Spirit refer to the soul, the body, and the Universal Energy or life force.

The Law of Three

Father	Son	Holy Spirit	Heaven
Soul	Body	Universal Energy	Earth

The Law of the Triangle

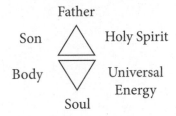

Father

Son   Holy Spirit

Body   Universal Energy

Soul

The Star of David

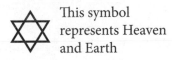

This symbol represents Heaven and Earth

It must be understood that the immortal soul enters the physical body at or before birth, and that spirit energy, life force, or Universal Energy is needed to help keep body and

---

1. Some of the background information in this chapter and in chapter 3 also appears, in a modified form, in my book *Ancient Teachings for Beginners*, published by Llewellyn Worldwide in 2000.

soul connected. This energy works like a magnet, maintaining the human soul within the physical form. Three essences are needed to manifest life: soul, body, and life force.

This Universal Energy is everywhere. It is in the air we breathe, the water we drink, and in all living things. Even rocks and trees contain this spirit energy. Without it, we and our world would not exist. It exists in Heaven as well and works its way down into our physical realm.

The same principle holds true at the time of death. As a person dies, the life force leaves the body and its quickly depleting aura, returning to the universe. When this energy leaves, the immortal soul cannot keep itself within the body, and journeys back to the heavenly fields shortly afterwards. Death has now occurred. This process repeats itself over and over until you eventually break the reincarnation cycle and return to the heavenly realms permanently.

There are two conditions that can affect this cycle of life and death in reincarnation. These conditions are called *karma* and *dharma*.

As used in Buddhism and Hinduism, karma refers to the actions taken by someone during a particular lifetime. These actions, good and bad, will sometimes determine that person's destiny in present or future incarnations. According to this belief, if you were cruel and abusive to your spouse in a previous lifetime, you would return in a future lifetime and possibly experience the roles in reverse, whereby your spouse would now be abusive toward you. For many people who are suffering hardship and trouble in this life, it may be because of actions from a past incarnation.

Recognizing this karma or karmic debt in your present lifetime and then changing your patterns now will result in a release of this debt. Realizing a past life can help you start to break the cycle of birth to rebirth because you have learned your lesson. This is part of your spiritual growth or evolution. The quicker you break or release these karmic debts, the quicker your soul growth and your return to the heavenly fields where you will remain.

Dharma, on the other hand, is just the opposite of karma. It specifically involves good thoughts and good actions. People who dedicate their lives to service to humanity are creating dharma, or "scoring points in Heaven."

Love and kindness shown to others will help you to break the cycle of reincarnation much faster than if you simply went through life doing nothing at all, simply coasting through this incarnation.

Dharma also represents a great cleansing to "wipe the slate clean" as they say. Karmic debt loads can be eliminated in a very short time when you help others unselfishly. Your motives should be pure and good.

With this understanding of karma, dharma, and the process of reincarnation, always be aware of your thoughts and actions and try not to judge others too harshly. Create thoughts of love and peace in your heart and mind. This will aid you in your spiritual growth, allowing you to become a better person and a kinder human soul.

Explore your past lives and learn who you truly are. Discover your past and embrace your present life. Reincarnation is the key that will open the door to the wonders and beauty of your eternal soul.

Also, know that as you explore your previous lives, angels and high-minded spirit guides will be there to help you on your spiritual journey. All of this will be covered in detail in chapter 3.

You are unique. You have chosen to return to Earth at a momentous time. You have a great opportunity to explore your previous lifetimes and allow your soul to become more enlightened. Delve into your past and enjoy your life here now on Earth.

Embrace the past, love the present, and cherish the future. You hold the key within. So, open the door and explore the wonders of your eternal soul.

Reincarnation and Past-Life Regression

Within this moment, the only moment that exists, the past, present, and future are contained.
—BUDDHA (CIRCA 563–483 BCE)

In a consoling letter to Elizabeth Hubbart on February 22, 1756, Benjamin Franklin wrote that the soul is immortal. The old boy was right. While on Earth, you are a soul living within a physical body, not just a physical body with a soul. The human body should be thought of as a temple or building that your eternal soul resides in temporarily while you are here in the physical. The body is merely the structure. When you die or pass over at the end of each of your earthly incarnations, and there are many incarnations, you as an eternal soul return to the heavenly fields above.

When you are "dead," commonly known as *in-between lives,* you can have some profound and wonderful experiences while in Heaven. This lovely realm or higher plane of existence contains beautiful gardens, teaching temples, and healing areas. During your time there, you will experience many events, heal your traumas received while on Earth, evaluate your last earthly existence, and eventually prepare to return to Earth.

Through my work with past-life regression, I've been repeatedly asked certain insightful questions about reincarnation and past-life regression. I pose them here for you, since I can only assume they will come up at some point in your own work.

Q & A

Q: If I am up in Heaven having a wonderful and peaceful time, why in hell would I want to come back to Earth?

A: Through past-life regression, a better understanding of your reincarnations—the birth, death, and rebirth process—can answer many questions that pertain to your reason for being here on Earth. As well, it can answer that nagging question "Why did I return to Earth in the first place?" It can help you understand why you came back. It helps you put both your life and your death into proper perspective. As a human soul, you are constantly learning and growing on your long journey back and forth between Heaven and Earth.

Many people say, "I didn't ask to be born." Actually, you did. You had a meeting or two with wise spiritual beings in Heaven. You made an agreement to come back to Earth. Many options were discussed with you. Finally, the right parents and the right country were arranged for you. You came back here to Earth to fulfill your contract with Heaven.

Q: How many past lives have I had?

A: After years of working as a past-life therapist, I have come to the following conclusion: there is no set number of past lives that you can have. Many people have lived numerous past lives here on Earth, while others have had only a dozen or so past-life experiences. It all depends on each person and their eternal soul. A human soul will keep coming back and experiencing the cycle of reincarnation until that soul has become enlightened enough to break this cycle of life, death, and rebirth. Finally, a human soul will return to Heaven and stay there after learning all the lessons that are necessary. So, a person may experience a dozen past lives or a hundred past lives or more! It all depends on the individual.

Reincarnation involves old souls and new souls. Old souls are human souls that have experienced many previous lifetimes on this planet. An old soul has lived dozens or more previous lives on the earth.

A new soul is a human soul that has experienced very few past lives on this planet. As new souls, they are newborn babes. Their wisdom, knowledge, and spirituality are not developed fully yet. They have not learned all the lessons necessary for their spiritual growth. Comprehension about deep philosophical subjects is lacking at first until these new souls grow and develop. Many new souls do not fully understand the world that we live in. Each of these souls will need many lifetimes in order to become more developed. For a new soul, this should be considered as a great opportunity to learn and grow on a spiritual level. The new soul may learn very quickly and become spiritually advanced in a very quick manner.

Old souls are more prevalent upon the planet. When you look into the eyes of a person who is an old soul, you will see wisdom there. It is easy to spot an old soul. The individual will be interested in many subjects and will embrace life upon the earth. There is a depth and an internal wisdom that shines forth from an old soul. Many of them will be very spiritual and caring. There is an inner knowing that they all possess. On a spiritual level, these old souls know why they are here and what they are supposed to do to make this planet a better place. These people understand what life is all about and recognize, on that same spiritual level, that they agreed to return to Earth for another incarnation.

Both old souls and new souls that learn quickly are here making a difference on Planet Earth. They understand life and death and strive to help others.

You will be able to tell an old soul from a new soul as you explore your own past lives. In any case, both old and new souls have great opportunities to grow and experience the wonders of this earth.

At this time on Earth, all souls have been given a great chance to achieve the greatest spiritual growth that is possible. All human souls have come back at a special moment in time to explore this wondrous possibility.

Q: Does past-life regression always involve traumatic events?

A: When you recall a past life, it does not always have to be painful. Some of the experiences can be joyful, uplifting, insightful, and, yes, even funny. Oh sure, you might encounter painful or traumatic events, such as being hanged as a horse thief. (Of course, not everyone was a king or queen in a past life.) But these situations help you to heal yourself on a physical, emotional, and spiritual level. These healing benefits far outweigh the negative aspects.

Some of your past-life encounters can be extremely funny. You do not always have to remember being burned at the stake as a witch, stabbed as a soldier, or persecuted harshly for your beliefs. Perhaps you might recall a peaceful, fulfilling lifetime as a farmer. Warm, pleasant feelings of raising crops and raising children could be the central theme of a particular incarnation. A lifetime of happiness may be presented to you. Through it all, it is a learning experience for your soul.

Q: When you reincarnate, do you always return into a human body? Can you come back as a dog or cat?

A: According to my own study and teaching, a human soul is a human soul. You always reincarnate as a human. The soul is eternal and attached to the heavenly fields above. When you die, your human soul vibrates on a higher frequency and returns to Heaven. You spend some time in Heaven and then you prepare to return to Earth once more.

You will repeat this process over and over. Eventually, when you are truly enlightened, you will no longer need to return to Earth. At that point, you have broken the birth-to-rebirth process or the cycle of reincarnation.

On the other hand, there is also something called the "transmigration of souls." Transmigration of souls means that a human soul can reincarnate into another animal such as a dog or a cat. Buddhists, followers of a religion embraced by millions, believe in this form of reincarnation. In other words, it is possible for a human soul to have been in the body of another being besides a human in a previous lifetime. This is one of the reasons that Buddhists around the world cherish and respect all life. Even a lowly insect is treated with respect. In our Western society, we might have a tendency to crush a spider that we find on our kitchen floor, but Buddhists would gently nudge the spider out the kitchen door instead of killing it. I suppose this is a very loving and peaceful way to look at our world. Although I believe that a human soul always reincarnates into a human body, lifetime after lifetime, one must, of course, have respect for other beliefs and religions. After all, we are all here on this earth to follow our spiritual path back to the Creator.

All of these varied religions and beliefs possess a truth and a spiritual essence.

Q: What previous lifetime affects me the greatest in this life?

A: It is your last two incarnations that have the greatest influences upon you. These two previous lifetimes are just below your consciousness waiting to be released. By meditating and using past-life recall techniques, you will pull one or both of these past lives to the surface of your conscious mind. Once you receive a glimpse of one of these incarnations, more and more glimpses will unfold.

Q: Have I always been a woman (or man) in my previous lives?

A: You will return to Earth lifetime after lifetime. Sometimes you might come back as a female; other times you will return as a male. This is part of the reincarnation experience. You might recall or receive only one or two lifetimes as a woman. In most of your recalls, you may be a man.

You may also return as a member of a different race. In one lifetime you might be a Native American; in the next you may be a Caucasian. This is normal.

Human souls can also reincarnate into different countries. For instance, I remember being an American born on the eastern coast around 1810. I was a writer and recalled memories from the American Civil War. In my present lifetime, I was born near Niagara Falls, Canada, in 1954. As a Canadian, I have feelings and emotions about both countries.

Q: What about my family? Is this my first life with them?

A: Families seem to reincarnate into family groups, incarnation after incarnation. In a past life, a person who is your sister now may have been your mother then. Relationship issues you had with that person in that lifetime may be brought forward into your current lifetime. It is during this lifetime that you must learn the lesson and break the karma or debt. This will allow your soul to move on.

When discussing families and reincarnation, another aspect needs to be covered. It is possible for someone's great-great-grandfather to return to this time period as the great-great-grandson. There was a program on television years ago about reincarnation. The name of the show escapes me, but it doesn't matter. In any event, in it a man recalled intimate information about a certain regiment of the Civil War. He knew all about the type of rifle used by the Union soldiers of that northern regiment. This man possessed detailed knowledge about this regiment, knowledge that he should not possess. Also, a picture of his great-great-grand-father was shown. The photograph looked very much like the great-great-grandson. In fact, the photograph of the great-great-grandfather looked like a twin to the descendant. This strongly suggests that many souls reincarnate into their family groups over and over.

Ways You May Experience Past Lives

You might be sitting in your kitchen, drinking a cup of coffee. You may be in a very relaxed state. Suddenly, a glimpse of you riding a white horse in the English countryside comes clearly into your mind. You can see how you are dressed. It is very vivid and very real for just a brief moment. Deep down inside, you know that you are seeing a bit of a past-life recall. With experience, you'll be able to recognize this more and more.

Once that happens, other scenes from that lifetime will start to come forward. You may start to see your home in England and beautiful flowers in a garden. Soon, more of this lifetime will be presented to you either in waking visions or while you sleep. Perhaps a vivid past-life dream from that time period will be shown to you in its entirety. You might even pick up your name and the date of this lifetime.

This lifetime that you are recalling is the one that is influencing you the most. Eventually, most of this previous embodiment will be given to you. It is your higher self that is working on your behalf. On a higher level you are remembering the past life that you need to see. This is always the case when it comes to reincarnation.

Another event that happens on a fairly regular basis is the quick flash or vision of a past life. This can often occur when someone is in a relaxed state. Many clients have told me that they were sitting in their kitchen or in their garden, just letting their mind drift. As this happened, all of them had quick visions of a previous incarnation. One of my clients remembered seeing himself sitting on a brown horse, dressed in a Roman uniform. He was looking down from a hill at the Roman soldiers marching along a roadway. As soon as he experienced this past-life glimpse, it ended abruptly.

Your angels and spirit guides will also be there to assist you as you explore your past lives. These wise and loving beings of light help open the doors to the past for you to see what you need to see. Always ask for their assistance as you explore your past incarnations.

Simultaneous Past-Life Recall

There is a very rare and special phenomenon that can occur in the past-life regression process. I call it *simultaneous past-life recall*. This sometimes happens when couples explore their respective past lives. When each couple is regressed to a previous lifetime, they will both experience the very same lifetime. For example, the husband will re-live the past life as a husband in a certain time period. He will recognize his current wife as his wife in that lifetime. All the scenes and events of that incarnation will play out for him. The same experience will happen to the wife. She will visit the same past life but as another person. She may be the wife back then and recognize her present spouse as her husband in that incarnation.

Storybook Past Life

People recall their own past lives in a few different ways. Sometimes a person will experience the past-life recall in the same format as a story. I call this the *storybook past life*. In it a person will have the past life unfold in chronological order. First, some may see themselves as small children. A special event might be seen and felt by them. Then, the past-life scene may move to a later time. In this case, the scene is of a young man or woman wearing old-style clothes. Several scenes of importance will be shown as the past life moves forward. Eventually, the individuals will see and even feel the pain and suffering of a death in that lifetime. As the past-life event ends, they will see themselves floating above the death scene. Some will experience the pain as they recall that time. Others will simply observe the death event. People experience past-life death scenes in different ways. Sometimes, due to the influence of the higher self, the individuals will revisit the pain and emotions. This happens in order to assist in the healing process of the soul. It helps the soul release the pain.

Bits-and-Pieces Recall

The next way that people recall past lives is a bit disjointed. I refer to it as *bits-and-pieces recall*. In these cases, the people undergoing a past-life recall will receive bits and pieces of past-life scenes and other information. These various scenes will be parts of one lifetime and then another. In many cases, people will see or feel memories from several past incarnations. For instance, a person may see himself as a pirate being hanged from the yardarm, and then the scene switches. Next, he may see himself as a farmer living in a green, peaceful valley. The past-life scenes or glimpses may flow into his mind very quickly. There may be a dozen or more scenes shown to the person.

This method does not happen as often as the traditional, or storybook, recall, but it does occur for whatever reason. The people can then analyze what they have experienced. Soon, more and more scenes or glimpses from some of these past lives will start to enter into the conscious minds of these people. One of these past lives may become dominant, and soon the whole past life is shown in its entirety.

People who recall past lives experience these events in two different ways. Some people will simply see the scenes unfolding. The individuals are observers to the event. They are watching the past life unfold as if they are watching a movie or television show.

Others will experience their past lives in a more intimate manner. When the past-life scenes start to unfold, the individuals will become part of the events. It is as if they are an actor within the play. They are there participating in the events and feeling all the emotions of that past life. To these people, it is very real. It can be quite traumatic. All the pain, sadness, joy, and other emotions are embraced by them. Their past-life death can be a trying event in some cases but not always. In some situations, the people will just float out of the body and observe the final moments from above. It does not always have to be an unsettling event.

No matter what happens, these past-life memories allow the soul to heal. An inner peace within may arise from this experience. The human soul retains memories, emotions, and pain from previous lifetimes. By recalling or re-living past lives, the soul can release these negative emotions and pains. The soul will then begin to heal. Both the physical body and the human soul can acquire emotional and physical trauma. The soul needs to heal the same as the body.

Past-Life Recognition

It is often said that the eyes are the windows of the soul. This is very true, especially when it comes to reincarnation. Let me explain. It is the eyes of the person that draw you in. On some level you recognize this person from another lifetime. Some people you develop an instant rapport with, although you just met the person, and you feel as if you have known him or her all your life.

Some of you may have an instant dislike for a person you have just met. Chances are you knew this individual in a previous lifetime. Maybe this person treated you badly in a past life. You may not remember any of that earlier lifetime, but your soul recognizes this other soul on some psychic or spiritual level. Again, the eyes may be the key. As you look into the eyes of this person, some feeling may be triggered within.

Repetitive Past-Life Dream

I had a client come to see me regarding a repetitive dream she had experienced for many years. She explained that in the dream she was standing in a lovely garden looking at a large, two-story white home. The home looked very familiar to her, and she felt quite comfortable in this dream. In the dream she saw herself enter the front doors of this house. Once inside she would explore each room and gaze at all of the furnishings. My client felt that the furniture, pictures, and other objects were from a time period in the 1800s. In her mind she felt herself touching many of the objects in the rooms. As she continued exploring, she would always end up in a bedroom on the second floor. Here she would gaze at the large bed, the pillows, and the curtains. She felt that this was her personal bedroom.

This dream that she had would be the same every time.

We talked about this repetitive dream. I told her that it was probably a past-life recall. When I regressed her back to a previous lifetime, she ended up in England around 1870. Sure enough, she saw the white two-story house. My client was able to recognize that she was a woman in that lifetime and was happily married.

Afterwards, she reflected upon this previous lifetime and realized that the repetitive dream was a past-life recall trying to come through to the surface. Everything made perfect sense to her.

Through the years, many of my clients have experienced similar events. All of them now recognize that they were seeing a part of a previous lifetime.

Future Life Progression

When you explore your past lives, you have the ability to go back in time and re-live a previous life. As an eternal soul, you also have the ability to receive visions of possible future events as well. This is sometimes referred to as a *future life progression*. You simply move ahead to events that will transpire in this lifetime or perhaps in a lifetime yet to come.

You can also develop the ability to meditate and focus on these future scenes. This can even happen during sleep. Allow yourself to experiment with future life progressions along with the past.

As you explore your own past lives, you will discover numerous things about yourself. You will understand who you are, where you came from, and, most importantly, why you are here on Earth at this momentous time. Soon, you will recall many past lives and develop or enhance more of your spiritual gifts and psychic abilities using the techniques within this book. As you explore the past, you will change your present and make your future better and brighter.

Allow your soul to be free, to feel the true eternal energy that flows within. Discover your past lives and embrace your future. I wish you all the best on your spiritual journey!

three

Angels, Spirit Guides, and Past-Life Regression

For He will give His angels charge concerning
you, to guard you in all your ways.
—Psalms 91:11

Angels and spirit guides have been part of our world for thousands of years. These beings of light have influenced many cultures, both past and present. They have helped to bring a part of Heaven to Earth.

These beings of love and light can also assist you with your own past-life regression work. They will guide you, comfort you, and help to heal you. When you are in an altered state of consciousness, angels and spirit guides sometimes will come to you and support you during your past-life regression experience.

Perhaps your guardian angel will hold your hand and walk with you as you explore a previous lifetime. Sometimes an angel or high-minded spirit guide will take you into a healing garden and communicate with you.

These celestial beings are with you while you sleep and in your astral travels into the heavenly realms. Simply ask for their help, and they will be there for you to help you on your past-life exploration.

What Angels, Spirit Guides, and High-Minded Light Figures Are

Many people confuse the terms *angels* and *spirit guides* when talking or thinking about these light beings. Countless numbers of people believe they are one and the same. Even though these beings work with each other and in some cases perform similar tasks or missions, they are not the same. Angels and spirit guides do not belong in the same phylum or order. The fact is that an angel has always been an angel and will always be one.

These celestial beings are the unique creation of the Creator. They have a divine connection with the Creator and perform numerous tasks on behalf of the heavenly realms. There is a hierarchy in Heaven that begins with God, the Creator, Supreme Being, Universal Energy, or whatever you wish to call it. It is here at the core or center that the Creator, consisting of both male and female principles, radiated divine energy outwards into the universe, the stars, the planets, and the earth. This divine essence possessing intelligence, power, and healing energy permeates both the higher spiritual vibrations of Heaven and the lower physical vibrations of Earth.

It is the angels that move and work in both realms. They are as numerous as the stars, are unique, and have different missions or purposes. Some of these special beings work as guardian angels, protecting individuals during their lifetimes. In fact, many small children can see their own guardian angels and accept these celestial beings with open and innocent hearts.

The hierarchy of Heaven consists of an established order of angels, starting with the archangels who possess wondrous powers and are responsible for all the other angels. The archangels are very close to the presence of the Creator and perform very special missions, taking on the attributes of important divine messengers, miracle workers, great healers, protectors, spiritual teachers, and warriors against the darkness of evil.

Unlike angels, spirit guides have existed in human form in the past. They have lived, felt, and experienced the emotions associated with living in the physical on Earth. These beings no longer possess a physical body and now function in their true essence as souls, possessing higher rates of vibrations than people do.

There is a very close relationship between the human family and spirit guides. Spirit guides, like human beings, come from "all walks of life." They have their unique personalities and idiosyncrasies, just as with human beings. They are merely souls without physical bodies who have agreed or wish to work with people. This service to humankind is provided for our benefit and so that spirit guides can grow and evolve toward their own true enlightenment.

High-minded light beings are beings possessing extremely high vibrations. Jesus, Saint Germaine, El Morya, Mother Mary, Buddha, and others are examples of these celestial beings that help humans.

They may exist in the heavenly realms but come down to Earth to assist humanity on a regular basis. All of these light beings possess amazing gifts.

How They Help Us and Why They Help Us

Angels can heal, comfort, protect, and guide you throughout your life. These spiritual beings are also heavenly messengers that herald news or bring warnings to people. The word *angel* comes from the Greek word *aggelos*, or *angelos*, which means "messenger."

Your angels will also work with you in strange and wondrous ways. Gifted healers or persons who have and desire to use this potential will be able to start working with healing angels.

These celestial beings possess healing gifts and can "vibrate down" from the higher realms or lower their frequencies, descending into this physical realm where they will join their energies with your auric field.

There are also angels assigned to people who are about to pass over to the other side. As the person's body is dying, the individual will start to see or sense the presence of angels, spirit guides, and loved ones. This visitation will normally occur a day or two before the death of the human body.

Spirit guides work in conjunction with the angels. Both share similarities with each other when assisting humans on the earthly plane. Spirit guides perform duties such as guiding, teaching, and comforting people.

Spirit guides, especially the ones in training, come here to learn and experience situations. All people have spirit guides around them as well as angels. And like angels, there are many types of these spirit beings or guides.

How You Might Experience Their Assistance

Certain spirit guides possess skills such as are found in physicians, healers, business managers, accountants, orators, teachers, and so forth. They will work specifically with individuals who need assistance in these distinct areas of expertise.

Some of you will have a few guides helping you at any one time. Others of you will have numerous guides around you to assist in your tasks and life experiences. Wise, loving teachers are assigned to many people in order to help them into more enlightened souls; many angels assist in these teachings as well.

There are some human souls in the heavenly fields who decide to become spirit guides rather than return physically to Earth; in some cases, these souls will be asked to work in this capacity.

All of this is pertinent to the soul growth of spirit guides and human beings as well.

Example of Working
with Angels and Religious Figures

Angela had been recently diagnosed with breast cancer. She called me and booked an appointment for some energy healing work. When she arrived, a scarf covered her bald head.

The loss of her hair had been due to the side effects of several rounds of chemotherapy treatment. I doubt if she was much older than her early forties.

Angela entered my office and sat down on the recliner. Since I could see the colors of the aura about her, I started "reading" this human energy field. All living things upon this earth possess an aura, or energy field. The light spectrum from the sun, the chemicals within the human body, the electromagnetic energy, the chemical secretions within, and the emotions all contribute to the aura of humans.

I glanced at the top of her head to see if there was any healing energy ready to work down into her aura and physical body. I then looked at her heart chakra and breast area. "Angela, I would like you to lift your arms up. I want to look under the arms," I said. Sometimes a person who has a cancer within the body, and is having chemotherapy treatments, will have certain colors swirling here. Usually, the area just over the lymph nodes in the armpits will have darker, uglier lights. I noticed on the right side in Angela's armpit, and into the right breast, an ugly grayish-green light. It floated just over the diseased area.

I explained it to Angela and told her what I saw.

As Angela put her arms back down and placed her hands loosely into her lap, she nodded and said, "Yes, that is where the cancer is. It's in my right breast."

Over the years, I have learned to interpret the colors in the human aura that cover the body and move about like the colors of a rainbow after a summer storm. With practice I am able to diagnose the health conditions of an individual. This is a gift that the Creator gave me in order to allow me to help people. In our world today there are millions of others with similar gifts. These people are sometimes called *medical intuitives*. Some of these special individuals can actually see within the physical body in much the same manner as an x-ray machine or other scanning device.

Others have the abilities to use empathic skills and sense where the problems are located within the human body. Many gifted healers are able to use this attribute.

Once I scanned Angela's aura, chakras, and her physical body, looking for any energy blocks and negative colors, I began the energy session. With a gentle voice I guided her into a very deep, receptive state. At the same time, the healing colors from above descended into her crown chakra, and moved downward into her energy field. These beautiful colors of light blue, light green, and white flowed over top of her physical form. These hues moved throughout each one of her chakras, especially her heart chakra or heart energy center. Then I was amazed as these healing lights moved into the right breast and under the arm into the armpit itself.

A peaceful smile graced Angela's face. In seconds, the lovely face of her guardian angel became superimposed there. The most incredible blue eyes stared at me, or rather through me. I felt like she was looking deep into my eternal soul. This was a profound and humbling experience for me.

I saw a shimmering light within her aura that started to move upward out the top of Angela's head. I knew that she was starting to soul journey or astral travel. The beautiful lights still danced and swirled around her.

With my voice I directed her to a peaceful garden. Then I asked, "Angela, tell me what you see. What is happening?"

"I'm floating through a lovely garden. I can see and smell the flowers here. I can also hear a waterfall splashing nearby. There are spirit guides who are covered in pretty lights around me. Someone, I think he is male, is holding my hand and walking me up some white marble steps. I'm staring at two brilliant golden doors. The reflection from the sun is almost blinding. My guide is pushing these large doors inwards. He is now looking at me and beckoning for me to follow him inside."

"Where are you?" I was very curious as I leaned forward.

"I'm standing inside the courtyard of a beautiful building. I think it's a healing temple. There are white marble columns surrounding the area where I am. A water fountain in the center is splashing softly. I can smell everything and feel the warm breeze here."

"How do you feel here?"

"I feel wonderful. I'm at peace here. I can feel an incredible amount of energy flowing through my body, especially into my right breast. It tingles in this area." Angela had a serene look upon her face. Her guardian angel was still gazing at me with those bright blue eyes.

"Just allow it to flow. Enjoy the energy. Describe what you see as well." I was watching the light show dancing around her. There were lots of green, blue, and white colors moving about. Over her right breast and under her arm, a great amount of these colors swirled. This was an indication that she was allowing true healing to occur.

"Oh! A beautiful woman dressed in a light-blue robe is walking toward me. I know who she is. She is Mary Magdalene, a great healer. She has a big smile on her face." Tears were slowly rolling down her cheeks as she stated this.

"Wonderful. Let the scene unfold." I was pleased with all that was taking place. I considered it a gift and blessing to be a witness to this wondrous event.

"I am lying above a patch of grass—just floating. There are huge shade trees above. I can see some sunlight shimmering through the branches. Mary is laying her hands on me. Some beings of light are joining her now. They are putting their hands on me. I can feel great amounts of energy flowing through me. It feels great. I'm sure these are healing angels working on me. All of them are concentrating on my right breast and upper arm. A cool tingling sensation is going into there."

It was best to let the events continue for a few minutes. She needed as much healing energy as possible. The ugly grayish-green color that was originally present over her right breast and armpit was changing to a lighter and prettier color. I noticed vibrant light green, light blue, and white energy swirling into this area. An amazing amount of this Divine Energy or Universal Energy was working into the breast, the tissue, and the cells. These healing colors from above were working right into the cellular level in order to heal the tumor. I knew something special was happening.

Angela was allowing her body to be healed. The angels, Mary Magdalene, and the Divine Intelligence from above were all working together in harmony. I thought of a symphony creating great music together. All were necessary to create the desired results. It was my hope for Angela that a true healing would be the result.

She described how Mary Magdalene and the healing angels worked on her soul form. Angela could still feel a tremendous energy flow.

"Now, they are finished. The angels are leaving. Mary is taking my hand and leading me to a stone bench. We're sitting there together. She is talking to me."

"Can you tell me what she is saying to you?" I was fascinated as I looked at her.

"Mary Magdalene is telling me that I am healed. My breast cancer was caught in the very early stages. She says that when you catch a disease at this stage, you have the ability to heal yourself if you believe. Mary and a few healing angels will continue to provide healing energy on me at nighttime while I'm sleeping. They will be doing this for several weeks. I've been given the opportunity to stay here on the earth for several more years. I am to make the best of it."

"Let the scenes continue. Ask Mary to let you see a previous lifetime, one that affects you now," I suggested gently to her, in hopes that she would also experience an important past life.

"Oh. Mary Magdalene is holding my hand. We are floating over hills and slowly descending to a beautiful forest. There is a large lake nearby. I can feel and see brown shoes on my feet as I am walking along a path. It is warm and peaceful here."

"Let yourself explore this place. Keep walking around and describe what you see and how you feel," I directed in a soft voice.

"I'm walking alongside the lake, and as I glance in the water I can see my face and what I'm wearing. My hair is brown and long. I'm quite pretty here. There is a light blue dress on my body. I must be around forty years of age."

"Allow it to continue. Let the next event unfold." I sat back and waited to hear what would happen next.

Angela's breathing started to get heavy. Her eyes were moving very rapidly back and forth under her closed eyelids. The peaceful look on her face had been replaced with worry and fear.

"I can hear the soldiers on horseback galloping toward me. I know they are after me. I'm very scared. There's no place to run. I'm trapped. I don't know what to do. I'm running away from the lake and into the forest. I hope I can lose them."

My client's breathing was still labored. Her face was twisted up as she continued with her tale. "No. Oh, no. I can see them now. They are on all sides of me. Some of them are riding their horses down from the hill on my left. The king's soldiers are everywhere. I'm surrounded. All of them are closing around me with their swords drawn. One of them, the leader, is yelling at me that I am an evil witch and must die. He says it is the king's orders that I and others like me must die. People like me are an affront to God-fearing people."

She continued, "I'm crying now and begging them to let me live, to leave me alone. I am innocent. I've done nothing wrong but heal with my hands and use herbs from the forest. They don't care. The leader is getting off his brown horse and walking toward me with his sword drawn. I can see the hate in his eyes."

I instructed Angela to allow the scene to continue and told her that her guardian angel was there protecting her. She was safe here as she watched the terrible event unfolding.

"He's stabbing me in the chest with his sword. The pain is horrible. It hurts so much. The front of my blue dress is covered with blood. I feel weak and I'm falling to the ground. My breathing is heavy. Blood is oozing from my mouth. I can see the soldiers looking down at me and laughing. I can see the blue sky and clouds just above. Everything is starting to go dark. I can feel a funny tug inside me."

"All right, Angela, I want you to see the final moments of that lifetime. Allow yourself to float above the scene and tell us what you see," I said. (I refer to "us" rather than "me" in these sessions, because I know that angels and spiritual helpers are also a part of all this.) I guided Angela with compassion, knowing that this moment was important for her in the healing process.

Her face became more relaxed as well as her breathing. "The pain is all gone. I'm floating above the forest and looking down at my dead body on the ground. I can see the blood all over the blue dress. The soldiers are starting to ride off. My fear is gone. I'm starting to feel better inside."

I leaned forward and said, "Move on from that lifetime. Go to a healing place. Tell us what is happening now."

"Mary Magdalene is back, and a beautiful angel is with her. They are both taking my hands and guiding me to a peaceful and pleasant garden. We are all sitting on the grass here holding hands. Mary is talking to me and telling me it was important for me to see this past life. She says that the sword stabbing my chest on the right side in that lifetime is partially related to the cancer in my right breast. Between the healing that she and the angels did on me and the release of this past incarnation, I am healing my body."

"Does she have any other messages to pass on to you?" I asked with great curiosity.

"Yes. She loves me very much and so do all my angels and spirit guides. She wants me to have a wonderful, long life. I'm to help others in any way I can. If all of us work together, we can heal this planet and create a heaven on Earth if we wish. She is giving me a big hug now and so is my angel. I think she is my guardian angel. They are smiling at me and waving goodbye. It is time for me to return to Earth now."

After hearing that, I guided Angela back and told her to focus on her body and the room. In a few moments, the colors around her decreased and she opened her eyes.

I asked her how she felt. Her reply was, "I feel great. I'm at peace. I don't feel so lost anymore. I know I'm being looked after. I also was told that the cancer is gone. I can still feel some tingling sensation in my right breast."

Angela left after thanking me for the session.

Many people have had similar experiences as Angela when they explore their own past lives. Mary Magdalene, the Master Jesus, and other religious figures will visit them and interact with them during their past-life recalls and astral visits to the heavens above. This type of event greatly enhances the person's past-life recall and affects each and every one of them for the rest of their lives. May we all be fortunate enough to experience the wisdom and healing from spirit helpers such as Mary Magdalene and other high-minded spirits.

Exercise: Connecting with Your Light Spirits

The following exercise is designed to help you connect with your angels and spirit guides. You can do this exercise anytime you want.

Begin by finding a quiet room to relax in. Try to remove excess sunlight from coming into the room. Put on some incense such as sandalwood or frankincense. Light a few white candles and place them in a few places throughout the room.

Now, find a nice, comfortable position to sit in; either a chair or the floor will work. Take a deep breath into your lungs and hold it for the count of five. Then release it slowly either through your mouth or nose. Take another breath in and hold it again for the count of five. Once again release all of the breath slowly and evenly out your mouth or nose. Then take another deep breath in for a third and final time. Again, hold it for the count of five and then release it slowly as before.

By taking in three deep breaths, holding them for the count of five, and finally releasing the breath slowly, you have relaxed your mind and slowed down your brainwave patterns. You have succeeded in placing yourself into a light alpha state of consciousness. This is the state needed to be able to connect with your light spirits.

The next thing to do is to ask for angels to come into your room for protection. Imagine the four corners of the room occupied by angels. Feel their presence and their unconditional love filling your heart and your room.

Now ask for spirit guides and high-minded spirits such as Buddha to enter the room. It is your choice whom you want to connect with. Some of you may want the strong, feminine energy associated with Mother Mary or Mary Magdalene to come to you. Feel their presence within the room.

As you are sitting there in a very calm and relaxed state, visualize or imagine one of these spirit guides floating just above your head. Take your hands and lift them above your head and then bring your hands slowly down. Let your hands move down both sides of your head, your neck, and then into your body. Once you have brought the hands down to around your shoulders, place them gently in your lap.

Wait a few moments and then repeat the technique, raising both hands above your head. As last time, bring your hands down past both sides of your head, past your neck, until you reach your shoulders. Finish this by putting your hands back into your lap.

There is one important thing you must do when you raise your hands above your head. Feel and sense the presence of a spirit guide or a high-minded spirit descending from above your head, into the top of your head or crown area. Feel this loving presence entering into your head and your body. You should feel a slight warmth or pressure on the top of your head as you do this. Also, you might feel a pleasant, cool sensation covering your face.

This is a sign that you have connected with one of your spirit guides or high-minded spirits. In essence, one of these light beings has descended into your aura, through the top of the head, and into your physical body. Just enjoy the experience for a few moments.

Let yourself relax and listen to any impressions or words that come into your head. If you have a question that needs answering, feel free to ask either with thought or with quiet words.

Know that the answer you seek will come to you sometime in the near future. You may get your answer when you least expect it while you are in an altered state.

Once you feel that you have experienced the connection with your spirit guide or high-minded spirit long enough, take in another deep breath and thank these beings of love and light for coming to you. Feel gratitude and love knowing that they have connected with you. Then imagine them leaving the room, but know that they can always come back to visit and communicate with you whenever you wish.

From this point, just return to normal breathing and extinguish the candles. Let yourself return to your normal life and go about your business.

Each time you attempt this exercise, you will notice more love and energy surrounding you and filling the room. You will start to experience more pleasant sensations on your head and face. This will help you to become more peaceful and awaken more of your spiritual gifts.

Angels and spirit guides are the bearers of love, light, comfort, and reassurance for many. Without these beings of love and light, our world would be a sad place of mere existence; no one would truly "live."

four

Meditative Techniques
That Encourage Past-Life Recall

Meditation helps you to grow your own intuitive faculty. It becomes very clear what is going to ful- fill you, what is going to help you flower.

—Osho (1931–90), Indian spiritual teacher

Now that you know about the basics of reincarnation and past lives, I want to focus on special techniques you can use to help you access your memories from previous lifetimes. The easiest way to begin to encourage past- life recall is through the use of meditation techniques. Here I include the more effective practices I share with my clients and students.

Many people are very visual. These individuals can see scenes unfolding in their minds in the same manner as watch- ing a movie. However, not everyone visualizes well. Some people will feel or sense impressions instead of seeing them. This is fine. You can still benefit from past-life recall if you feel and sense emotions and other things. Eventually, as you explore your previous lifetimes, a *window* will open up in your mind. All of a sudden you will become visual as well. Meditation is one of the tools you can use to achieve this result.

Another great tool to use is memory. For instance, if you want to visualize yourself standing around a campfire, let your memory be your guide. Remember when you went camping as a child, and someone built a roaring fire in front of which you stood? See yourself there and feel the warmth of the comforting fire. Hear the wood crackling and see the various colored flames glowing within the fire. This will help you to awaken your visualizing skills. Use this technique whenever you need to. It doesn't always have to be a huge fire. Perhaps you can remember being on the beach on a warm summer day where you can feel and smell the breeze. Let yourself experiment with memories of your past. Again, triggering your memories from earlier in this incarnation will allow you to open up and visualize in an easy manner.

Out of all your senses, smell is the strongest one. This holds true in the psychic and spiritual realms. Through the years, numerous clients and students have remarked how strong their sense of smell was when they experienced a past-life recall. Some of them have smelled smoke, various kinds of incense, body odors, flowers, and much more. This allows the individual to visualize past-life scenes unfolding in their minds.

Buy different types of incense and essential oils. Try them out and see what happens. Sandalwood, frankincense, and myrrh are great ones to try. By burning incense you will also help to raise the vibrations within the area. This ensures that higher spirit guides and angels are drawn there. Also, feel love in your heart. This has a tendency to bring in angels as well. Let yourself drift with these wonderful smells.

The Meditation for Beginners exercise just below involves the use of imagination. This exercise was designed to help you awaken your imaginative skills and eventually develop your abilities to visualize easily.

Visualization and Using Other Senses
Meditation for Beginners exercise

Learning to meditate effectively on a regular basis is the initial key needed to access your past lives. When you learn to meditate, you can slow down your brainwave patterns and place yourself into a lightly altered state of consciousness. The various states of altered consciousness will be discussed in the next chapter. It is very easy to learn to meditate. All it takes is practice and concentration.

Breathing is a main component of proper meditation. The breath is very important in the process. Let us begin by practicing a simple breathing exercise.

First of all, find a quiet and private place. Make sure that there are no sounds, noises, or other distractions that will interfere with your meditation. That includes turning off your cell phone or disconnecting a telephone.

Sit down on the floor, grass, or in a comfortable chair. Now, take in a deep breath through your nose and hold it for the count of five. Then release it slowly out your mouth or nose. This is your choice. Focus on the breath as it slowly leaves your body. Feel your lungs releasing this vital air as you do this.

Wait a few seconds and then repeat the process. Take a deep breath into the lungs and hold it for the count of five. Again, release it slowly out your mouth or nose and focus on the breath leaving. Let your mind go quiet as you release the breath this time. By allowing your mind to go quiet or drift, you can enter easily into an altered state of consciousness. In other words, you zone out. This helps you to begin receiving glimpses or pictures of previous incarnations.

Repeat the exact breathing process a third and final time. Feel the breath going into your lungs. After the count of five, release the breath slowly out the nose or mouth. Focus all your attention on the breath as it leaves your lungs and is released into the air.

Now, return to normal breathing and focus on your chest as it rises and falls with a gentle movement. Keep focusing on the breath going in and out of your lungs for a few moments.

At this point, you have already begun to slow down the brainwave patterns and placed yourself into a lightly altered state of consciousness.

Next, find something directly in front of your eyes to gaze at. If you are outside, perhaps you can stare at a cloud drifting by or at a tree. If you are inside, stare at a picture on the wall or at the wall itself. As you keep staring at the object that is directly in your line of vision, start to stare through the cloud, tree, or picture. Imagine that you are looking right through the object, as if you are looking past it into the distance. Continue doing this for several moments. Just let your mind drift as you do this. Try not to think of anything in particular. Just relax and let your thoughts come on their own. This helps you remain in a slightly deeper altered state of consciousness for a bit longer.

Enjoy the relaxation and peace as you sit there staring off into space. After a few moments of this, you are ready to finish the technique.

Simply take another deep breath into the lungs and hold it for the count of five, the same way that you began the meditation. Then release the breath slowly out your nose or mouth. Feel and focus on the breath as it is expelled.

Repeat the process a second time in the very same manner. Allow the breath deep into your lungs, hold it for the count of five, and then expel it slowly as before.

Complete the Meditation for Beginners technique by repeating the process a third time. Once you have released all of your breath out of your lungs, resume normal breathing. Let your eyes return to normal viewing. Stop staring off into space and start looking around your environment in a normal way.

You should feel relaxed and peaceful after doing the Meditation for Beginners technique. Your brainwave patterns are still slowed down a bit. You are still in a slightly altered state of consciousness.

After you have practiced this technique a few times, you can add one more thing to it. Next time you are trying the meditation technique, instead of letting your mind drift, allow your imagination to take over. Imagine that you are in ancient Rome walking through the Roman Forum, or in ancient Athens standing on a hill in front of the Parthenon.

Create or imagine a scene from an ancient land and focus on it. Let yourself daydream. This part of the meditation technique will help you to awaken your visualization abilities. If you already visualize quite well, this exercise will enhance it even more. When you can easily imagine yourself walking through parts of ancient Rome or Greece, you will be able to see yourself existing in a past life more easily.

Deep Meditation

Through deep meditation you can recall past lives and even receive visions of the future.

The following special exercises are given to you to help you slow down your brainwave patterns and ultimately meditate effectively. This will allow you to enter into deep states of altered consciousness. The more you practice these techniques, the deeper you will go. Eventually, you will enter into a mid-to-deep-level alpha state and you will achieve this state in a very quick and profound manner. These techniques can help develop the ability to meditate deeply due to the fact that you are in a very deep altered state. This is a marvelous gift. Deep meditation allows you to slow down your breathing and your brainwave patterns, and release tension and stress. We can all use a little stress reduction in our lives nowadays.

There are other methods available to assist you in attaining deep meditative states. Visit bookstores and metaphysical gift stores. Peruse their selections of meditation DVDs and meditation CDs. Some meditation CDs are specifically designed to guide you to recall your past lives. Any meditation CDs that are designed to work on your chakras—the energy centers that connect the physical body with the energetic body—are also very effective. These energy centers are closely connected to the endocrine glandular system and affect it in a positive way. When you work on your own chakras and open all seven of these major energy centers, the chi, or Universal Energy, will flow through these centers.

This energy, along with your own chakra energy referred to as *kundalini*, will also flow up and down through your body, allowing your body to relax deeply and your brainwaves to slow down dramatically. Your soul may start to slip out of the physical body. It may enter into an in-between state referred to as the *bardo state*. This means that your soul has left your body and hovers just above your physical form. When you are in this state of being, you may start to recall a past life in a very clear and concise manner.

As a past-life therapist, I employ a special chakra meditation to assist clients to recall past lives. In technical terms, this technique is called an *induction method*. Simply put, the client is induced into the proper altered state in order to help him or her experience a past-life recall.

The Chakra Flow Meditation or Induction Technique

In my book *Ancient Healing Techniques*, I describe this technique in detail. This exercise can be used for two reasons: to recall past lives and to astral travel. For simplicity's sake, a shorter and altered version of the Chakra Flow meditation will be explained to you here.

The human chakra system contains seven major chakras, or energy centers. There are also roughly 120 minor chakras positioned throughout the body. Your hands, knees, and feet possess some of these minor energy centers. By accessing these centers, you can begin the chakra-flow energy process.

Begin by adjusting the lighting in the room to resemble a near-dusk environment. Next, find a comfortable chair or sofa to relax upon. As soon as you are in a relaxed position, take in a deep breath, hold it for a few moments, and then release all of the breath either through your mouth or nose. Repeat the process once more. Then take a third and final deep breath into the lungs. Again, hold the breath for a few seconds. Finally, release it all slowly through your nose or mouth. Return to normal breathing and let your mind drift.

The next step is to take your hand and place three fingers onto the top of your head in the crown chakra area. Hold the fingers there and focus on the pressure and sensations. Then put your hand back into your lap or by your side. Now, focus all your attention on the crown chakra and imagine a warm sensation like the sun penetrating through the top of your head. Concentrate on this area for a brief moment.

Then take your hand and touch your forehead with two fingers in the third-eye area. Feel the pressure or sensations from your fingers. Remove your fingers after a moment and place your hand into a relaxing position either in your lap or by your side. Imagine a warm purple flame burning about an inch below the surface of the brow. Feel it expanding all the way across your forehead.

Then, touch your throat with two fingers and feel the slight pressure there. This is where the throat chakra is located. Remove your fingers and put your hand back into your lap or by your side. Focus on warmth from the sun penetrating through here. Let it spread all the way across your throat. Even let the warmth penetrate deep into the throat and neck.

Next, place your hand over the middle of your chest in the heart-chakra area. As you do, take a deep breath into your lungs, hold it for a few seconds, and then release it slowly either through your nose or mouth. Immediately after this, focus on the warmth and pressure of your hand upon your chest. Imagine a small fire underneath, deep within your chest. Just feel the warmth and pleasant sensations flowing across your chest. This indicates that your heart chakra is opening up and releasing energy through this area. Enjoy the pleasant sensation here as you continue to breathe in a normal but relaxed manner.

As you do this, you can also think of someone you love very much. This will increase the energy in the heart chakra. This allows warm, loving energy to flow through the heart chakra and into the body. Soon you should feel even more warmth in the middle of your chest.

After a few more moments, remove your hand from the heart chakra and move it to the solar-plexus chakra, which is about one or two inches above the navel.

As you lay your outstretched hand here, focus on it. Take a deep breath into your diaphragm this time. You should feel your stomach and hand lifting slightly as the vital breath goes into this area of your body, the lower part of the lungs.

Release the breath slowly in the same manner as you did the last time. From this point, just concentrate on your hand and solar plexus. Feel the warm energy from your hand starting to penetrate through the surface. (Remember to keep your eyes shut during this meditation.) Visualize a warm fire burning just under your hand. Feel the warmth here increasing and let it spread across the solar-plexus chakra. Allow the sensation to work deep into the stomach and internal organs. Concentrate on this for a few moments.

Now, move your hand down to just about one or two inches below your navel. Lay it gently upon this area, the sacral chakra. Take a deep breath into the diaphragm and feel as if the air, filled with chi, has entered into the sacral chakra. Hold the breath for a few seconds and then release it slowly through your nose or mouth in the same way as last time.

Return to normal breathing and focus on your hand and sacral chakra. Feel the warmth and energy from your hand working into the muscles and internal organs directly below your hand. Again, imagine a fire, this time an orange flame burning within. Let the flame or fire spread throughout the sacral chakra. Allow the warmth and energy to radiate deep into the lower back and hips. Focus and enjoy these sensations for a few moments.

When ready, place your hand over your base chakra in front of your body about two inches above this area. Feel the warmth of a red fire or flame burning in the reproductive organs. Let it spread across the base chakra and into the hips. Imagine the warmth of the sun or the flame warming this whole area. Even feel the warm sensation radiating deep into your hips, buttocks, and tailbone. Concentrate on this pleasant energy for a few minutes.

Leave your hand on top of the base or sacral chakra. In your mind, see yourself moving warm water or a warm flame up from your base chakra into your sacral chakra. Once you have the energy there, focus on it for a few seconds. Then, continue to move that warm water or fire up over the navel into the solar plexus. Again, feel the pleasant energy here for a few seconds. Allow this warmth to spread completely across your solar plexus and enjoy the warmth in the pit of your stomach. Focus on the solar-plexus chakra for a moment or two and then let the warm energy move up over the breast and into your chest. Again, visualize someone you love and let this added warmth spread across your chest and into both breasts. Enjoy this pleasant, warm sensation as it spreads throughout the heart chakra and the area around it.

After a few moments, let the warm fire or water move up into your throat and feel a slightly warm sensation there. Continue to move this warm energy up over your mouth, your face, and your eyes. Let the flame or water flow upward into the forehead or brow. Feel the warm sensation here, especially in the middle of your forehead. Remember the slight pressure you felt as you placed two fingers here the first time. Focus on this and the warm flame or water as it spreads across the brow from temple to temple. In your mind, see a purple flame burning in this area about an inch below the surface of the skin. Concentrate on this feeling for a few moments.

Then, when you are ready, see and feel yourself moving the warm flame or water up to the top of the head in the crown chakra. If you need to, touch the top of your head with three fingers again in order to revive the slight pressure or sensation you felt there originally. If you decide to use your fingers at this point, just put them there for only a second or two. Then place your hand back into your lap or beside you.

Now, imagine yourself outside on a warm summer day. Feel the heat of the sun beating down upon your bare head. Let this warmth penetrate deeply into the top of your head. Let this warmth spread downward and throughout all of the upper part of your head. You can also picture a warm yellow flame burning within your brain. Just concentrate on your head and your brain. Imagine the warm energy working completely through your brain. Feel the warmth on the top, sides, and back of your head.

From this point, start moving this warm energy back down through your body and chakras. Think of it as "connecting the dots." Feel it as one fluid motion of water or fire moving downward. Allow it to flow down your face, past your throat, and into your chest. Let it spread across this area. Feel the warmth deep inside as the heart chakra is activated even more.

Next, move the warm flow of water or fire over the breast and into the solar-plexus chakra. Let this warm energy spread completely across your stomach. If you wish, put a hand there in order to help you focus. Feel the slight pressure and warmth of your hand. This will add to the exercise.

Let the warm, pleasant sensation continue to move like a flow of water downward over the navel and into the sacral chakra. Allow the water or flame to spread across this energy center from hip to hip. Enjoy this wonderful and relaxing sensation.

From here, move the warmth down into the base or root chakra. Feel the warm energy there. Allow it to spread across from thigh to thigh. Concentrate on it and let this warmth penetrate deeply into the base chakra and ultimately the hips and buttocks. Even feel a warm sensation in your tailbone.

Now, move the warm energy back up your spine and the front of your body. Imagine this energy as warm water or sunshine moving gently up your body. When the energy gets to the top of your head, begin again.

From here, move the energy back down through your body. Feel it as one fluid motion flowing down your face and the back of your head, past your throat and neck, through your chest, and even down the middle of your back at the same time. Let the fluid sensation of warm water or fire continue flowing down into the solar-plexus chakra, the sacral chakra, and into the base chakra.

Once you get the energy to this chakra, move it back up the body and through all the other energy centers again. Feel it moving slightly faster as it works upward through the body and chakras. Feel a warm sensation moving up your spine at the same time. Let the energy continue flowing up over your face and into the crown chakra at the top of your head. Feel a warm energy or tingling sensation moving up your upper back, over your scalp, and into the crown at the same time.

From here, let the warm energy move back down through your body and all the chakras again. As it gets to the base, let it flow back up into the crown chakra.

Move this chakra energy up and down the body several times. Then, let it flow on its own. Do not direct it at this point. Just allow this warm, pleasing energy to continue flowing up and down through the body, the chakras, and the spine, muscles, and nerves. Allow it to keep flowing on its own accord a few times.

When you are ready, concentrate on the warm water or fire again. Direct it up and down the body and through all the energy centers. As you do, start to slow the flow down. Make it continue to slow down even more. Finally, stop the flow, either in your crown chakra or heart chakra. This is your choice.

Once you have finished the Chakra Flow meditation, just relax and let your mind drift. You may receive past-life recall at this stage. There is a very good chance that you will start to receive past-life visions or memories while you attempt this chakra-flow exercise.

In any event, enjoy the experience. Practice it as often as you like. The more you practice, the more adept you will become at doing chakra energy work. You will start to astral travel and enjoy past-life events unfolding in your mind. You might even visit the Akashic Records, or Universal Library, and access some of your past lives. This will be discussed in chapter 9, "Astral Travel and Past-Life Recall."

Some of you may have a problem relaxing. Perhaps you find it difficult to meditate. The following suggestion might help: take up Tai Chi or yoga as a form of exercise. Both of these modalities are very beneficial in slowing down your brainwave patterns, thus allowing you to relax. If you practice one of these modalities, not only will you be able to learn to meditate, but you will also get in touch with the energy within your body. There are some individuals who are what I refer to as "natural energy feelers." These people feel the chi, or energy, easily inside their bodies. They are adept at moving this energy through their bodies like a flow of water. Others may need to work at it.

When you become familiar with Tai Chi movements or yoga poses and positions, you will learn to move this chi throughout your body as well. Once you have become conversant at this, you can attempt the Chakra Flow meditation with greater results.

By relaxing, meditating, and letting chakra energy or chi flow through your body, you will be able to start to recall past lives.

When you meditate, you allow your soul to explore. You link with your angels and spirit guides. Wonderful messages of hope and inspiration can be passed on to you by these beings of love and light. Sometimes they will use humor in their messages and in their actions. When you become adept at meditation, you will slow down your breathing dramatically. Again, your brainwave patterns will also slow down, allowing your mind to become quiet. It is in this state of relaxation that visions, inspirational ideas, and past-life experiences will come to you.

In some cases, you may even hear or sense spirit guides and beings of light communicating with you. Your soul is more attuned to all of this. You are more closely connected to Heaven above.

Through deep meditation, you can lift the veil and see into your past. As I've stated, visions, scenes, and feelings of previous incarnations can be shown to you. It may appear as a movie unfolding upon your mind. This is a great gift to develop. Enjoy it and explore.

Allow your mind and your eternal soul to be free and to experience many of your past incarnations. This will help you in your spiritual growth.

five

Past-Life Recall Techniques

Yea, I am one with all I see,
With wind and rain, and pine and palm;
Their very elements in me
Are fused to make me what I am.
Through me their common life-stream flows,
And when I yield this human breath,
In leaf and blossom, bud and rose,
Live on I will… There is no Death.
　　　—ROBERT W. SERVICE (1874–1958), POET

Now that you have beginning tools that encourage past-life recall, I want to focus on special techniques you can use to build from there. These techniques can be used in safety in the privacy of your own home to recall your own past lives.

These techniques are designed for everyone, from the neophyte to the more advanced student. No matter what level you are at, these exercises and techniques will prove valuable to you. If you are already starting to explore your past lives, doing these several exercises will enhance your abilities. As I briefly mentioned before, this is partly due to your brainwave activity.

The human brain can generate as many as ten watts of electrical power. It has four brainwave patterns. These brainwave patterns are known as *beta*, *alpha*, *theta*, and *delta*.

The first brainwave pattern, beta, operates between fifteen and forty cycles per second. This is considered the alert or waking state. When your brain operates at a beta level, you are wide awake, focused, and possibly working. This is the state that most of us are in during our waking state of consciousness.

Alpha, the second brainwave pattern, operates between nine and fourteen cycles per second. This is considered a relaxed state of consciousness. When you lie down or relax in a comfortable chair for a few moments, your brainwave patterns automatically slow down from a beta pattern to this alpha pattern or state. This is an important state of consciousness that we will discuss very shortly.

The next brainwave pattern is the theta state. This is a state of very relaxed and drowsy feelings. This pattern functions between five and eight cycles per second. When you are in this state of relaxed consciousness, you can start to manifest visions and past-life recalls.

The final brainwave pattern is the delta state. It operates at one and a half to four cycles per second. It is considered the sleep state in which you dream. It is a very deep state of consciousness where you can also recall past lives. This state occurs in a lucid or past-life dream. (Some lucid dreams are past-life dreams.)

Your brainwave patterns must be altered or slowed down in order to become receptive to past-life impressions and memories. There are several exercises or techniques that you can use to slow down your own brainwave patterns, especially from a beta to an alpha state.

The Chi Deep-Breathing Exercise and May Chant

Start by finding a peaceful and private place to do this exercise. If you are at work and have a few moments available, you can even do this at your workspace if you wish. You want to be left alone and uninterrupted for a few minutes while you do this special breathing exercise.

First, relax yourself by taking a deep breath into your lungs and diaphragm, and holding it for about five to ten seconds. It is important to draw air into *all parts* of your lungs, not just the upper part of your lungs. Then, release your breath slowly and evenly, either through your nose or your mouth. This is your choice. Now, take in another deep breath and repeat the process. Do it once again with a third and final deep breath. When you do deep breathing three times and hold the breath in, the chi or Universal Energy (also called life force) contained around you in the air is drawn into your lungs. As this breath containing the chi is held within, it helps to expand and cleanse your auric field. Your brainwave patterns will slow down, allowing you to enter into a more relaxed state.

Now, take in one more deep breath, hold it for a few seconds, and then begin to release it. As you do, chant

M-M-A-A-Y-Y evenly and strongly until your breath is completely exhaled. (If you are at work, you might want to do the chant very quietly. There is no reason to have your co-workers look at you in a strange manner!) This chant should be attempted in a mid-C musical note, approximately. If you are not musically inclined, do not worry. Simply find a scale or sound not too high and not too low, but in-between, a midpoint. Repeat the May chant once more, letting yourself feel the vibration working from your third eye or brow area into the middle of the head, and finally up toward the top of the head, where the crown chakra is located.

Repeat this a third and final time, allowing the sound to work throughout the head. Many of you will feel the "tingles" on the top of the head or other parts of the head. Some of you will feel lightheaded. These are indications that the pituitary gland and surrounding areas of the brain are being affected. This gland is indirectly connected to the crown chakra. The crown chakra opens up, allowing you access to the Creator or Godsource. This also helps to open your psychic and spiritual abilities. This includes lifting the veil from the past and letting you start to receive past-life memories.

When you chant May as described above, you will send a vibration deep into your head. This vibration will affect the pituitary gland profoundly, allowing it to activate. This in turn opens up and activates the crown chakra, which is indirectly connected to the pituitary, as already stated. As the crown chakra opens up fully, psychic impressions and high energy from the heavens above enter through this chakra into the top of the head. This energy will trigger electrical impulses within the brain and release these impulses through neurons in the brain. As these neurons fire, areas of your brain that contain dormant psychic gifts will reawaken. Again, you may feel tingling sensations all over the top of your head. This is an indication that the chant has worked properly. Soon, more psychic and spiritual attributes will unfold. One of these many gifts involves past-life recall flowing into your conscious mind. A flood of past-life memories and emotions may be the result. These memories may continue to invade your conscious thoughts for several months as these formerly dormant areas of the brain awaken fully.

Incidentally, the pituitary gland is not just a physical gland but a psychic gland as well. This gland has the potential to receive high vibrations of spiritual and psychic energy from above. This very high energy will vibrate down into a lower frequency, where the human brain assimilates this information into an accessible message.

It is important that three breaths are taken in, held for about five to ten seconds, and then slowly released. Three is a magical and mystical number. Three represents completion, and involves the Law of Three or the Law of the Triangle (see chapter 1).

This law is in direct reference to the chi or Universal Energy that is everywhere, which surrounds you and is in the air that you breathe. It also involves reincarnation and the Holy Trinity.

The chi or Universal Energy held in your breath consists of two elements: *positive essence* and *negative essence*. This is based on the same principle as the Law of Magnetism and the Law of Electricity. Both the negative and positive elements or polarities are important and of equal value. One needs the other, and they work in harmony together.

It is through the process of proper deep breathing, along with specific breath-holding techniques, that your lungs draw in the required amount of Universal Energy needed to revitalize and sustain your physical form. Practicing the Chi Deep-Breathing exercise on a daily basis greatly assists in slowing down the aging process. It will also slow down your brainwave patterns in a quick manner, allowing you to contemplate on previous lifetimes. You will enter into a light or medium alpha state and become receptive to past-life recall.

Proper breathing techniques are important. Most individuals have a tendency to breathe in a shallow manner. If you can get into the habit of taking in deeper breaths, your health and energy level will improve.

A form of these breathing exercises can be done in the morning and at night just prior to going to bed. Stand by a window that is slightly open, even if it is winter and it is cold outside. Now, as you stand near the window, take a deep breath into your lungs and hold it for about five to ten seconds. Then release the breath slowly either through your mouth or nose. Repeat the deep breathing once more and hold it again for the same amount of time. Release it all again. Then repeat this breathing exercise a third and final time. Once you have expelled all the breath out of your lungs, return to normal breathing and go back to what you were doing, or head off to bed if it is nighttime.

This deep-breathing exercise pulls more Universal Energy into your body. This improves your health and slows down the brainwave patterns into a light alpha state. This makes you more receptive to receiving past-life impressions.

Past-Life Contemplation Exercise

This exercise is a very easy and relaxing method to explore your past lives. It is designed for you to employ in your own private and quiet space. A bedroom or a quiet place in your home is the best venue for this exercise.

Begin by lighting a few white candles within this private room. Put on some incense as well. Sandalwood, frankincense, and myrrh are three of the best ones to use. Smell is a powerful tool that can be used to recall past-life memories and feelings. By using lighted candles and incense in the room, you will also raise the vibrations, allowing angels and high-minded spirit guides to enter into this area.

Now, find a comfortable place to sit or lie down. The Chi Deep-Breathing exercise should be employed. You do not have to chant May at this time. Simply doing the breathing exercise will be sufficient. Once you have expelled your breath after the third deep-breathing attempt, relax and let your mind drift. As you do this, keep focusing on your breath rising and falling in your chest. Do this for a few moments. Then gaze toward the wall facing you if you are in a sitting position, or gaze at the ceiling above you if you are lying down. Just keep staring through the wall or ceiling and continue to allow your mind to drift. Do not focus on anything in particular. After a few minutes of this, you are ready for the next phase. Now, say to yourself, "I want to recall a past life. I want to remember a past life." Then let the thought go. At this point you can either leave your eyes open, staring at the wall or ceiling, or just close them.

It is crucial that you do the next thing. Let your imagination take over. Imagine that you are in an ancient country. Perhaps you are walking through the Roman Forum, looking at the stone buildings and various people, or you are floating down the Nile on a boat. Let yourself watch the palm trees moving gently in the breeze along the shore. Just let your imagination flow.

Imagination is a very great gift. It is the key. When you use your imagination, you let your visualization abilities come to the surface. Many people also feel and smell things associated with previous lifetimes. By using your imagination, you can awaken the ability to visualize or see things, such as glimpses from previous lifetimes. Once your visualization skills open up, you will be able to recall past lives more easily and with greater clarity. When that happens, you can visualize, sense, and feel many events from past lives.

Enjoy the experience!

As you do this exercise, there is a very good chance the images in your imagination will switch over to actual visions of a previous embodiment. One moment you will be walking through the Roman Forum, and the next, you will be in another place, such as France. The vision will continue to unfold. Maybe you will see your life there as a merchant or a young woman. Scenes will start to materialize where you may see buildings and people. You might even smell certain smells such as flowers or trees. Just drift and let the scenes continue.

By using your imagination at the start, you have opened up other areas of your brain. The imagined scenes will change over to an actual past-life recall. You can use the Past-Life Contemplation exercise whenever you wish. The more you practice this exercise, the more past lives you will recall. You will become adept at this, and even start to receive past-life pictures while in a waking state. You might be sitting outside in a garden, relaxing and enjoying the day, and suddenly a past-life scene will flash before your eyes. This is an indication that you have lifted the veil that hides the past and revealed some of your incarnations.

Candle and Mirror Technique

This particular technique or exercise should be practiced in a room that has limited light. Nighttime is preferable, but you can simulate this by closing curtains and blinds.

Once you have created a nighttime environment, take two white or light candles and place them on a dresser or platform standing in front of a large mirror. Light both candles and position them on either side of the mirror out of your direct line of sight. Gaze at your reflection, noticing where there is too much shadow on your face. Adjust the candles to remove as much of the shadow as possible and to allow the candle light to show your head, face, and shoulders clearly reflected in the mirror.

After the candles have been positioned properly, start gazing into your eyes in the reflection. As you do this, let your gaze "look through" your eyes. Take deep, relaxing breaths. Three or four deep breaths should be sufficient. Remember to breathe in through your nose, filling both your chest and abdomen, and then let your breath out slowly, either through your mouth or nose. After three or four deep breaths, return to normal breathing again, still staring through your eyes into the distance. Your eyes and face may start to shift and change at this time. For example, your nose may look as though it is getting longer or your eyes might start to look different. This is expected as you enter into a deeper state of consciousness.

You are now in the proper altered state. Bring your focus back from staring "through your eyes" to staring at them, allowing your mind to drift as you do so. As you continue to gaze at your eyes, a few things will occur. In a moment or two you will start to notice your face altering and shifting. You may notice that your face looks older; your nose may be longer; and another face looks back at you. You may see the visage of a wizened Asian man gazing back at you. This face may appear as an overlay on top of your own face. As soon as you focus on this image, it may change and become the face of a young, beautiful woman looking back at you.

You may experience these facial shifts five or six times. Each time a new face will gaze at you. Some of these faces will look very familiar to you. In essence, you are looking at several of your own faces from previous lifetimes. They may appear as male or female, different nationalities, and different ages. Just keep looking and enjoy the various visages as they appear in front of your eyes.

You might also notice that one of the faces takes precedence and continues to gaze back at you. These facial features may continue to be there for several moments. If this happens, take advantage of this opportunity. Just gaze through this facial feature. Soon you may start to receive visions of that particular lifetime. Scenes of Japanese gardens or a tropical island may come into your mind. Keep doing this for a few more minutes. Finally, when you have gazed at the face from one of your past lives for a while, the image will fade and then you will simply be looking at yourself once more. Just enjoy this experience and contemplate upon it afterwards. When you do, more insight and information will be given to you.

Try the Candle and Mirror technique several times a week if you wish. The more you practice this technique, the more past-life information you will receive. You have effectively lifted that veil that descends upon the human soul at the time of birth. Explore your many past lives and allow yourself to grow spiritually.

Mutual Face-Gazing Technique

This technique is pleasant and enjoyable. Instead of using the Candle and Mirror technique, find a partner or friend to practice face-gazing. Ensure that the room is in a near-dusk environment or is completely dark with only a few candles to light it, enough for you and your partner to see each other adequately.

Both of you should sit in comfortable positions facing each other, with about five feet of distance between you. Take a few deep breaths in and out, relaxing yourselves. Then just start gazing through each other's eyes in the same manner as you did in the Candle and Mirror technique.

In essence, you and your friend are substituting the mirror-gazing with each other's faces. Simply do the same thing with each other's faces as you did with the Candle and Mirror technique.

If you are successful, you will see the facial changes upon each other's faces as you enter into deep altered states.

Continue gazing at each other's eyes and faces for some time. Observe how you feel within and what you sense and see upon each other's faces. The energy in the room should feel peaceful and pleasant. Finally, when you and your partner have experimented long enough, take in a deep breath and hold it for a few seconds, then release it slowly. Let yourselves come back to normal awareness.

This enjoyable technique can be done whenever you wish, provided necessary precautions have been taken to ensure that you, your partner, and the room are peaceful. The room should be quiet, with all unwanted sounds kept out of the space.

Glass of Water and White Light Technique

The following technique is very powerful and effective in recalling past lives. Start by filling a glass with water and taking it into your bedroom or a place where you are going to lie down. Sit down and take a deep breath in, holding it in for a few seconds. Then release your breath slowly either through your nose or mouth. Take in a second deep breath and repeat the process. Finally, take in a breath a third time and hold it again for a few seconds. Then release all of your breath slowly through your nose or mouth once again. After this point, return to normal breathing and allow your mind to remain calm.

Next, take the glass of water and place it between the palms of your hands. Let your hands completely encircle the glass. Hold the glass of water and gaze into it. Focus on your hands and fingers. Soon you will feel and sense the blood flowing into both hands, including the fingers and thumbs. Let it continue. In a few moments you will begin to feel your hands starting to pulse or throb. It will feel like a strong heart pulse as you concentrate on it. Allow it to get stronger. At some point, your hands will feel as if they are trying to push away from the glass. This is normal. It is a sign that the energy within the glass of water is changing; it is being magnetized.

The Universal Energy, spirit energy, or chi is everywhere, and this energy exists in two essences, positive and negative. Both the positive and negative essences make up the complete Universal Energy.

The human body possesses this energy in both positive and negative states. The right side of the body contains more positive energy, while the left side of the body contains more negative energy or essence. When you place your hands together as you hold a glass of water, the right hand will send positive essence into the water by way of the palms, fingertips, and thumbs. The left hand will send negative essence into the glass of water in the very same way. Under the Law of Magnetism, positive energy draws negative energy toward it, while positive polarity to positive polarity repels. Also, negative essence or polarity repels negative polarity. It is quite simple when you think about it.

As you hold the glass of water between your hands, the positive essence of the right hand and the negative essence of the left hand will flow unimpeded into the water. Again, positive and negative attract each other. In about five minutes the glass of water will become charged or magnetized. The warmth in the hands and the pulsing sensations existing between them are indications that the water has been charged. At this point, drink the glass of water down. This will send the charged water into your physical form.

The magnetized or charged water changes the polarity of your body and soul in this manner. Normally, your physical body possesses a negative essence while your eternal soul possesses a positive essence or polarity. Under the Law of Magnetism, like repels like, and unlike attracts unlike. So, as the energized water enters your physical body, it helps to make your body more positive. When this occurs, a more positive-oriented body will repel a positive-oriented soul. This allows the human soul to leave the physical form more easily.

After drinking the charged water, lie down on your bed. Shut your eyes and take a few deep breaths in and out. Return to normal breathing and keep your eyes shut. In your mind, visualize a white light surrounding your bed and then another white light surrounding you and your bedroom.

The white light you visualized surrounding your bedroom and your bed puts you into a protective space. It ensures that nothing of a negative nature such as a lower entity will be able to enter your bedroom and interrupt your past-life dream.

As you continue to lie there, say to yourself, "I want to remember a past life. I want to remember a past life." Then just relax, allowing yourself to drift into a light sleep. As you do this, imagine that you are walking in an ancient town. Then let yourself go to sleep.

If you are successful, you will experience a very lucid and vivid dream, which is actually a past life remembered. Enjoy the scenes and just be part of the internal movie.

When the soul leaves or astral travels, it will often go to the Akashic Records, or Universal Library (discussed in chapter 9). While here, it will open up and explore your own personal soul records. In your soul records are kept all of your previous lifetimes. One or more of your past lives will then unfold in a lucid dream form. Please note that some lucid dreams are past-life dreams, but not all lucid dreams are past-life dreams. Some lucid dreams may be you traveling in your soul form as well.

If you are experiencing a past-life dream, it will appear very real to you. At some level you will know that this is a past life being shown to you. The information and scenes will be very specific regarding a previous lifetime. If you are astral traveling, the scenes and experiences will also be very real for you, but without the past life being shown.

The next morning after you awaken, write the event down in a notebook or journal. Keep the journal in a drawer near your bed. You will find through the years that you will be able to add other past-life dreams and memories to your journal.

Try the Glass of Water and White Light technique about once a week. The more you attempt this unique technique, the greater chance you will have of succeeding in recalling one or more past incarnations.

Keep practicing these techniques. You will awaken more of your spiritual and psychic abilities. As these gifts open up more, you will become adept at recalling past lives. So, visit the past and know that you have lived before. When you have experienced these techniques and feel ready to move on to more advanced exploration, move on to chapter 6. You will find the following techniques a bit more challenging. They are designed to help you explore your past lives successfully. Enjoy the techniques.

six

More Advanced
Past-Life Recall Techniques

The more you learn to link the use of breath, mind,
and voice, the greater your own power in life.
—TED ANDREWS, AUTHOR AND SPIRITUAL TEACHER

The ancients believed in the duality of the universe. There was the macrocosm as reflected in the heavens and the stars, and the microcosm as reflected in the earth and in nature. They also believed that this duality existed in human beings; we possess both a physical body and a psychic body. The difference was that the psychic body was contained within the physical body, but it manifested at a much higher vibration than its physical "shell." Accordingly, along with physical organs there were in fact psychic organs residing within the human form.

Everything in nature is surrounded by energy patterns. Trees, plants, and animals all possess energy patterns or radiations of multicolored lights. Humans are no exception.

An amazing energy field surrounds the human body; this is often referred to as the aura, the electromagnetic field, or the human energy field.

Within the aura are energy centers called *chakras*. In Sanskrit, the word *chakra* means "wheel of light." As I mentioned in chapter 4, there are seven major chakras and about 120 minor chakras contained within the human aura. All of these chakras are indirectly connected to certain parts of the physical body by way of the aura and psychic body. These centers are located above and around areas of the body and exist at a very high frequency or rate of vibration.

The primary chakras are indirectly linked to the major glands of the endocrine system by way of the sympathetic nervous system and the central nervous system. These chakras are located up and down the body, from the head to the reproductive organs. Again, these major chakras are the crown chakra above the top of the head, the third-eye chakra in the brow area, the throat chakra in the throat area, the heart chakra in the middle of the chest, the solar-plexus chakra about an inch above the navel, the sacral chakra just below the navel, and the base or root chakra in the base of the spine.

Awakening the abilities to recall past lives involves this human chakra system. All seven of these chakras are important in order to open your psychic and spiritual abilities and be able to recall your previous incarnations.

Now, it is the crown chakra and the third-eye chakra that we will be focusing on specifically with regard to past-life recall techniques. In the last chapter we covered the crown chakra in the Chi Deep-Breathing exercise and May chant. I explained that this technique is designed to allow you to open up your crown and access psychic information from the heavens above. This also includes receiving knowledge from your angels and spirit guides. In some cases, these beings of light will pass on information about your past lives and grant you visions of these past incarnations.

The Advanced Third-Eye Technique

The following technique is very important. It is designed to awaken your psychic gifts in a profound manner. It is also a more advanced technique to aid you in recalling your past lives.

You will learn ancient techniques to awaken, or more accurately, reawaken the third eye, one of the primary energy centers in the psychic body. Once this is accomplished, you will be further on your path toward psychic enhancement and spiritual growth.

When the term *third eye* is used, it refers to the sixth chakra, or third-eye chakra, located in the center of the forehead. It is closely associated with the pineal gland, which is also considered to be a psychic gland. Lying within the brain, this particular gland remains mysterious to medical science. Nevertheless, scientists agree that the pineal gland functions as an internal clock in some way, and that it is affected indirectly by light. As darkness approaches, it activates the release of a hormone called melatonin; when daylight arrives, the secretion of this hormone ceases.

The pineal gland is actually a part of the endocrine glandular system of the body. The term *endocrine* comes from the Greek words *endo*, which means "inside" or "within," and *krinein*, which means "to separate." These glands release certain hormones directly into the bloodstream of the body. All the glands of the endocrine system work in harmony with one another.

The pineal gland is also believed to be associated with reproduction and works in conjunction with the pituitary gland as well as the hypothalamus region of the brain. The pineal gland has been misnamed; it is actually an organ.

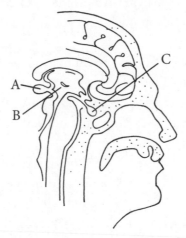

A=Pineal, B=Hypothalamus, C=Pituitary

As children, our pineal glands function properly, allowing us to use our intuition, creativity, and psychic abilities freely.

Usually around the age of twelve, many children start to lose some of their psychic abilities, not because of puberty but because our society discourages their use. Our educational system emphasizes logical thinking and analysis.

Many parents, educators, authority figures, and other adults discourage children from using their psychic abilities by dismissing them as imaginative or by accusing the child of making up stories. This closed-minded attitude causes irreparable damage to many young gifted children. Under these conditions, the pineal gland becomes atrophied and begins to calcify as less energy is directed there. This major physical change in the pineal causes the loss of psychic and spiritual abilities. The ability to recall past lives is also affected in a negative way. By age twenty, many young adults are unable to use these abilities.

Fortunately, our society is becoming more open-minded and tolerant toward the psychic and spiritual side of life. This more enlightened attitude helps to keep the pineal gland activated and the third-eye chakra functioning well. The third eye, which is directly affected by the activated pineal gland, will in turn activate or "open up" and allow people of the light to shine forth in a spiritually evolving world.

The concept behind the third-eye technique is to create a vibration within the head, specifically within the pineal gland and the area surrounding it.

What is the source of this vibration? It is derived from the power of words produced by the human voice. The proper tone induced by a voice can create an energy or vibration that profoundly affects the human brain. The method is sometimes referred to as toning, chanting, or "doing vibrational work."

By chanting a specific sound based on a certain musical note, a vibration or sound movement can be triggered within the pineal.

This third-eye exercise creates a vibration or pressure in your jaw and face, causing this vibration or energy to work its way into the pineal gland. This vibrational energy triggers a resonating effect upon the pineal and activates it.

The intonation or chant to use is *Thoh*. *Thoh* rhymes with "toe" and is pronounced just as it appears. It is chanted in one syllable using a mid-to-high C musical note. Again, if you are not musically inclined, do not worry about attaining the exact frequency; an approximation is just as effective. Just remember that the proper sound is an alto note, midrange between a deep bass note and a high tenor note. In other words, to attain the right vibration, you simply chant *Thoh*, not in a deep low voice and not in a high voice, but between both of these ranges.

To begin the exercise, take in a deep breath through your nose and hold is as long as is comfortable, then slowly release it through slightly parted lips. Repeat this twice more. This breathing technique allows you to pull vital life energy or Universal Energy into your lungs and then into your whole body. It also slows down your brainwave patterns from beta level or waking state to a light alpha state, an altered state of consciousness. The alpha brainwave pattern is the state where meditation begins. You become more relaxed, making it easier to concentrate on the intonation of *Thoh*.

Next, take in another deep breath through your nose and hold it for a few seconds. Just before you release your breath through your mouth, place your tongue through slightly parted teeth. Put a light pressure onto the tongue with your teeth. This is the same process as saying the "th" part of "the." Once the tongue is in this position, release your breath through your mouth saying *T-H-H-O-H-H* until all your air has been expelled. You should feel the air moving past your tongue and teeth. If this technique is done properly, you will also experience a pressure or sensation in your jaw and cheeks.

Repeat this technique twice with a few moments' rest in between each chant. The Thoh chant should be said three times in succession in the first attempt. About twenty-four hours later, repeat the chanting technique in the same manner, saying *Thoh* three times with a slight interval between each chant.

This exercise should be done one more time, about twenty-four hours after the second try. This third day of saying the chant *Thoh* should be the final time. This is a one-time technique that does not have to be performed over and over like most exercises. If you wish to experiment with this exercise once more, try it about a month later.

For some of you, this ancient technique that has been passed down through the centuries may not seem to have any effect at first. Do not worry, as the effects of this exercise can be very subtle. You may have many physical and psychic experiences within a short period of time, or such experiences may not manifest for several weeks.

Physical Effects Resulting from the Third-Eye Technique

One of the first experiences that you may have is a headache or pressure in the center of the forehead, just above the brow. This sensation may feel like it is originating from within, usually an inch or more below the surface of the forehead. This is an indication that the pineal gland is reactivating and starting to function in a healthy manner. Some people, whose pineal gland is completely atrophied, may experience a migraine headache lasting a few hours. This discomfort can occur within a few days or a few weeks after the completion of the third-eye exercise. For most, the headache or pressure will be considerably less. The severity of the side effect is totally dependent on whether the pineal gland is fully functioning or completely atrophied before you begin the exercise.

For some, the sensation may even be pleasing. If you do not feel anything, try the technique a month later.

After the occurrence of the headache or pressure in the forehead, you may wake up one morning feeling a throbbing or tingling sensation in your forehead; it may feel like a goose bump. When this happens, the feeling may be so intense that you will look in a mirror to see what is there, but there will be nothing to see. Your forehead will look as it should. However, the strange sensation of pulsing or throbbing will continue through most of the day. This is the final physiological effect that you will experience after the third-eye exercise. It indicates that your pineal gland is once more fully awakened, activated, and functioning as it did when you were a child. As your pineal gland activates and balances itself, the rest of your endocrine glandular system will become more balanced and operate more harmoniously.

Eventually, this strange sensation will stop. You may find yourself becoming more lightheaded on occasion and start daydreaming more. For those of you who already do a lot of daydreaming or drifting, this change of awareness may not be noticed as much. The daydreaming and light-headedness means that your brainwave patterns are changing, slowing down. Instead of functioning and working in a normal waking state (i.e., using a beta brainwave pattern during the day), you are starting to operate in an alpha brainwave pattern or, more accurately, a light trance state. This state of consciousness is the state you should be in during most of your day. A person works more effectively, can handle more stress, and finds that time flows more quickly while in this altered state.

Eventually, you will find a balance between the beta state and the alpha state and daydream less often. No one will notice that you are working and living your life in an altered state of consciousness.

Incidentally, you are now using more of your brain's immense capacity.

Psychic Effects Resulting from the Third-Eye Technique

The third-eye chakra starts to activate and "open up" once the pineal gland has been activated. On a psychic level, the results are as follows:

- Intuitive abilities increase
- Creativity expands
- Clairvoyant abilities develop

- Empathic abilities increase
- Ability to see and sense auras obtained
- Clairaudient gifts develop
- Past-life recall and memories awakened

These gifts and abilities will start to unfold as your third eye opens. The third-eye technique is a powerful and effective way to develop your psychic abilities. It will also lift the veil that descends at birth, allowing you to see many of your past lives.

The third-eye technique is a key to increased psychic development and spiritual enlightenment. With the awakening of your pineal gland and your third-eye chakra, you will step onto your path, pointed in your life's true direction. The recall of some of your past lives is a great part of this spiritual journey.

The Resonance Method

Using the resonance method is another very effective technique that works to open up more of your mental capacity and allow for greater past-life recall. It is called the *resonance method* because you are resonating with objects around you and applying the method to past-life regression.

This exercise allows you to open up more of your mind to receive more past-life glimpses.

Look around you; observe what you have in your home. What type of furniture or accessories do you like? What types of movies and television shows do you enjoy? Is there a place or two in the world that fascinates you? Perhaps you want to visit these places or already have in this lifetime.

For instance, I know a few individuals who have Victorian-era furniture and antiques in their homes. These people love to watch movies and television programs about Great Britain during that time period. A few of these individuals have traveled to Britain on a few occasions in order to see the architecture and scenery. It is interesting to note that they have made comments such as "I felt like I was at home when I was over there."

This is a prime example of people who have a strong connection to that place and time due to a past life experienced there. A few of them might even remember a memory of that previous embodiment. If these individuals were to focus on their trips and contemplate the places they visited, they might start to remember scenes from that previous lifetime.

Several individuals I have met through the years have told me about their experiences while traveling overseas. When they visited a particular site and relaxed there, suddenly scenes of a lifetime in that area started to show up in their mind. Strong visions and emotions were evoked by simply being in an area where they lived in a previous time.

So, if you are drawn to a particular place, such as Italy for example, make arrangements to visit this lovely and historic country. You may very well experience a powerful past-life recall there. The veil that slams down upon you when you are born can be lifted, and a wonderful vision may unfold. Soon, more scenes from that former lifetime will enter into your conscious mind. Once this occurs, more past lives will start to come to you either in a relaxed state or while you are asleep. Your lucid dreams will actually be past-life dreams.

If you enjoy watching shows or movies about ancient Rome or Jerusalem, then try the following experiment. Watch an archaeological show or a historical program about one of these cities. Then retire to bed. Just before you fall asleep, contemplate on the show that you have just watched. Finally, let your mind drift. Let yourself daydream. Now, just as you are about to fall asleep, say to yourself, "I want to recall a past life there. I want to remember a past life."

From that point, allow yourself to drift off to sleep. During the night you might have a past-life dream in a very lucid way. The dream will appear very real to you with some detail. When you wake up in the morning, write down all that you remember about that vivid dream. This will help you to open up more of your psychic abilities. You may even start to recall more of that lifetime that you dreamt about. Eventually, all of that lifetime will be presented to you in stages. Maybe while you are relaxing and sitting in a quiet place, a clear vision from that previous incarnation will unfold upon your mental screen.

One final thing you can attempt is to hold a piece of jewelry or other accessory from that lifetime in your hands. Touch it and let your mind drift. Soon you might receive a quick vision of someone or something from that time period. Just relax and let your mind wander. Always remember that you are eternal and that you have lived upon this wonderful planet many times before. Your soul holds the key! Know yourself and discover your true spiritual path. Discovering your hidden abilities and past lives can be extremely rewarding, no matter how challenging the experience.

Examples of Past-Life Recall

The soul comes from without into the human body, as into a temporary abode, and it goes out of it anew...it passes into other habitations, for the soul is immortal.

—RALPH WALDO EMERSON (1803–82)

For many years I have worked as a past-life therapist as well as a medical intuitive and spiritual teacher. Countless individuals from many walks of life have come through my doors seeking spiritual direction, guidance, and the recall of previous lifetimes.

Through it all, many of my clients have experienced interesting previous lives. These experiences have been profound and in some situations life-changing for them. I consider it a gift, a wonderful treasure, to be a witness to these events.

In this chapter I will be detailing some of the case studies or past-life experiences a few of my clients have had. Some are funny and some are not, but in each recall, the client received the information that he or she needed. The individual's higher self takes over and guides them to what they need to see, feel, and experience. As I said earlier, sometimes an individual with a physical or emotional problem will be able to see where the problem arose from and release it. Some clients then heal themselves by experiencing the past-life recall.

Physical pain, unfounded fears or phobias, and deep-seated anger can all be traced back to previous embodiments. Our traits, our characteristics, our idiosyncrasies, and our unexplained physical and emotional pains can be traced back as well. Some of the gifts we have are brought forward from the past. Even some of our likes and dislikes can come from our former incarnations. I share these stories for your own benefit in your own experience of past-life regression. Through reading these examples, you will become more aware of your own past lives and be prepared to accept even more past-life experiences.

I feel strongly that these case studies need to be included here. Reading these reincarnation stories experienced by some of my clients will let you know how powerful, profound, and in many cases life-changing the results of recalling past lives can be. Reading these stories shows that you also can revisit your own past lives in a similar manner.

In the following case studies or past-life stories I have changed the names of all of the clients who experienced these interesting past-life recalls. I hope you enjoy each of these stories.

Unexplained Physical Pain

The following story is about a client who was not only a regular, everyday person previously but also a very crude and earthy individual. She was anything but ordinary.

Jane came to see me for regression therapy on several occasions over a six-month period. She was one of those special individuals who are easily hypnotized.

Through deep-breathing techniques, Jane relaxed very quickly. Her closed eyes started to move around—a sign of rapid eye movement, or REM. This was an indication that she was in a properly altered state of consciousness.

Jane began talking in what sounded like an Irish accent. "I can see everything around me. Ooy. 'Tis a beautiful day."

At this point I thought it was the proper time to ask her what she was standing on. This is a technique I often employ to get my clients to focus on things around them.

"What are you standing on?" I inquired.

"I'm standing in a pile of sheet," Jane replied.

"Pardon me. Please, could you repeat that?"

"I said I am standing in a pile of sheet. I am out by the barns," she answered.

"Oh," came my reply.

Jane continued. "It is a beautiful day. I think I will go to town for a pint."

As she kept talking, it became obvious that she was a man in this lifetime. Alec was the name of the individual. He was described as short and stocky with balding hair.

Alec seemed to be quite the character as he detailed his life and what he did. He had a wild sense of humor and loved to drink. He had no problem chasing the ladies either, although he was married. Alec commented on this. "Variety is good for ya. Besides, I'm a horny old goat."

Jane, now Alec, continued his story. He described the beautiful hills and trees in the late springtime. Soon he was walking into town and heading straight for the local pub on the main street. It was his home away from home, as he put it.

He walked through the entrance doors and found a seat behind an old and scarred wooden table. He described the inside of this drinking establishment to me as he kept talking. Alec had a pint of ale followed by several others. It wasn't long before he was feeling the effects of the ale.

"Aye. I'm three sheets to the wind," he announced. A funny, contented smile graced the face of my client as she sat there in a deep, relaxed state.

Soon Alec described how he got to his feet and unsteadily walked out the front door of his local pub. He exclaimed how he felt slightly blinded by the bright sunlight as it assailed him. He stepped off the sidewalk onto the cobblestone street in a bit of a drunken state.

Alec looked to the right down the main street. At the bottom was a park with a stream flowing through it. A beautiful young woman was there, bending over to examine a flower.

The inebriated Alec bellowed, "Oooh. What a lovely lass. I love the way she's bending over." It was at this moment that he first heard and then felt something hit him and knock him down. Briefly, Alec described the last moments of that lifetime. A beer wagon had run him over. The wheels went over his hips, crushing him. He recalled floating above the scene.

"I always knew the liquor and the women would be the death of me. Damn beer wagon." This was the last comment he made.

My client started to stir out of her altered state. I guided her back to the present. Jane opened her eyes and looked about. She smiled at me.

I decided to ask her if she remembered everything in her past-life recall. (In some cases a person will not remember all of it.) Her answer was yes, she remembered it all vividly. It was just like it happened yesterday.

Jane explained to me that she had problems with her hips and lower back for years. In fact, the discomfort plagued her and often it was debilitating. Shortly after this past-life session, she noticed that a great deal of her pain had disappeared. The past-life trauma of being run over by a beer wagon had been brought forward into this lifetime. By recalling the scene vividly, she was able to release the deeply buried pain.

So, if you are experiencing certain pains in your body that medical science cannot find a physical reason for, perhaps you should consider exploring a past life. It doesn't mean you were run over by a beer wagon in the past. The past-life event might be something that is less dramatic, such as falling off a hill and injuring your back.

As human beings we are complicated and wondrous. Our minds can open up the past for us, heal the traumas, and affect our present in a positive way. Jane was able to release a physical pain by recalling this previous lifetime.

A similar situation of unexplained physical pain occurred with Henry. He suffered greatly with severe headaches. The pain was so intense and long-lasting that he was considered a disabled student. For years he had attempted to pursue his intellectual studies in hopes of completing his university degree. Unfortunately, he was unable to achieve his goal due to this terrible affliction. In desperation he came to see me for a past-life regression.

It is not unusual for someone to seek out complementary or alternative healing modalities, especially after an exhaustive search of mainstream medical treatments has been unsuccessful.

When Henry arrived for his initial past-life session, he was in between bouts of intense pain. Through a special guided meditation or induction that involves chakra or energy-flow techniques, he was able to enter into a deep, altered state of consciousness.

After a moment of quiet, I asked Henry to describe what he felt and saw. The following story unfolded. He explained that he lived and worked as a slave on a plantation. The location was somewhere in the southern United States, although he was not sure of the exact whereabouts.

"What is your name?" I asked quietly a few moments later.

"My name is Eli," came the reply.

Henry, or rather Eli, continued to describe his incarnation. He was twelve years old. It was warm and humid as he worked in a field alongside other slaves. A large white house stood in the distance, where Master W lived with his family.

One day, as he walked past the house with its imposing white columns, he noticed a young white girl sitting on a swing in the front yard. She talked to him briefly and said her name was Melissa. The relaxed expression on my client's face changed slightly when he mentioned this chance meeting.

"Master W is mad," explained Eli. The owner of the plantation had found out about this brief encounter and was angry. The end result was that Eli was whipped for this slight transgression. Through the ordeal this twelve-year-old boy did not cry too loudly. He explained that if he had, he would have been beaten worse.

Later, Eli lay on the wooden floor in his family's home, a shack. It was then that the young slave started to sob. Jed, his father, was chastising him for talking to the white folk.

My client Henry was now sobbing. His prone body twitched a bit. He seemed somewhat uncomfortable being in a prone position upon the couch.

I decided to move him ahead to a later period in that particular incarnation. I gently guided him with my voice using a breathing technique. Henry's body became more relaxed, and soon another scene unfolded.

It was ten years later, and Eli was a young man with powerful muscles. The years of hard work in the fields of the plantation had contributed greatly to his physique. He was on the run during the time of the American Civil War. Caring people associated with the Underground Railroad were helping him to escape to the north to freedom.

By pre-arrangement he met the Adamson family, who were traveling in that direction in a covered wagon. The father, a gray-haired man, along with his teenage son quickly stowed Eli into a hidden compartment directly beneath the floor of their wagon. This is one of many ways that people working with the Underground Railroad helped runaway slaves.

As they attempted to cross from the Confederacy into the Union side, the family was stopped. Confederate soldiers on horseback surrounded the wagon. Eli could hear all of them asking questions about runaway slaves. Racial slurs and derogatory comments escaped from the lips of many of the soldiers. There was some yelling and swearing. According to the young fugitive, soldiers were ready to kill any runaways.

Finally, Eli felt the wagon lurch forward, and the angry voices grew dimmer. He heard a few gunshots in the distance.

Again, I instructed Henry to move forward to the final moments of that lifetime. In great detail he discussed the final scene.

"I'm workin' for the Union," Eli said with pride in his voice.

Then he described the place where he lived and worked. It was a big northern city by the sea. The young man, now free, was working outside of a warehouse, loading supply wagons. He was well liked by many of the Union soldiers stationed there.

Eli kept lifting heavy parcels and placing them onto the wagons. As he did, a group of Confederate prisoners went by, escorted by guards. He stated that some of the prisoners glared at him.

Suddenly, a scuffle broke out between the blue-uniformed guards and their prisoners. One of the Union soldiers who knew Eli yelled back at the young freed slave. "Eli! Help! Come quickly!"

The former slave dropped his parcel and ran toward the melee. The soldier who had summoned him struggled with a Confederate officer. Eli grabbed the rebel soldier's arm.

"Keep your filthy hands off of me!" screamed the officer. Then he produced a gun that was hidden away and put it to the side of Eli's head.

In an instant, the freed man felt a horrible pain and saw a flash of light within his head. He described falling to the ground mortally wounded. After that, Eli felt himself drifting above the terrible scene.

During this final moment, the moment of death in that previous existence, my client moaned and became totally still. Henry's breathing started to slow down. His rapid eye movements ceased.

I then used a special guided technique to bring Henry back into the present time. This technique also involved helping his soul to return into the physical form. This process took a minute or two. When he opened his eyes, he seemed more rested. My client told me he felt overwhelmed with the experience but felt it was a positive one.

I did not hear from Henry for about a year. One day he phoned me out of the blue. Henry proceeded to tell me that he no longer suffered from debilitating headaches and was working on his university degree. He explained to me in a very excited manner that his past-life regression had helped him greatly. Also, he had followed up his session with several Reiki treatments. The energy-healing sessions had also assisted him tremendously. Henry was now meditating on a regular basis. He informed me that the combination of all of these modalities had resulted in a cure. That was the last time I heard from him.

Years later someone mentioned to me that Henry had completed his university studies and now lived a more productive life free of pain. I hope and believe he is living life to the fullest and contributing to the betterment of our world.

Obviously, Henry was healed from a physical pain. The debilitating headaches that he had suffered from for years finally disappeared. This shows one of the healing benefits that can be received through accessing past-life memories.

Traits and Characteristics

Tom came to see me for a past-life regression. He was doing this simply out of curiosity. He was excited about the chance to recall a previous incarnation.

When Tom lay down on the bed in order to get ready for the session, he explained to me that he was very tired and hoped he would not fall asleep through it all. I told him not to worry, and then I proceeded to guide him into the proper state. He was a very easy person to work with and relaxed quite easily.

My client talked on a constant basis during the roughly two-hour session. A vivid tale unfolded.

Tom very quickly started to describe a scene out of ancient Rome. He explained who he was and what he did for a living. "My name is Naphro. I am a master craftsman," he proudly exclaimed.

"Can you tell us where you are right now?" I asked, leaning forward.

"I'm inside the administrative building of the town. There are lots of marble columns and a marble floor with mosaic designs on it. On the wall in front of me I can see the name of the town."

"What does it read?" was the question I directed to him.

"Herculaneum. That is the name of my town." Tom, or rather Naphro, quickly replied.

I leaned back in my chair and let my client continue with the story of that lifetime.

Naphro described the interior of the building in great detail. He then left this structure, turned left, and headed up a cobblestone street. There were old one- and two-story buildings on each side as he walked up the street, which inclined upward. A man driving a cart full of amphorae came down the street, and Naphro stepped aside as it passed.

Naphro continued his stroll until he spotted a bar that opened onto the street directly ahead on his right. The door and window were open. There was a stone counter in the open window area. Some pots of food were sitting in holes that were built into the counter. Behind the counter a short, bald man wearing a brown tunic stood. A dirty brown apron covered his rotund belly. Several chairs and tables were within this drinking establishment. According to my client, the fellow looked like a shifty character as he wandered about with a wine jug in his hands. A dirty towel with fly specks on it hung over his arm.

Naphro stopped at the bar, or *caupona* as it was called, and had a cup of wine. He stood on the street and leaned against the counter.

"How does the wine taste?" I asked with curiosity.

"It's been watered down. Cheap bastard!" was his reply. "It tastes like some animal pissed in it."

After finishing his fine wine, Naphro continued on his way. He then described something else a few seconds later. "I'm passing by the iron gates of the governor's house on my right side. A soldier with a spear is guarding the front. The house is very beautiful inside. There is a lot of beautiful furniture and expensive possessions inside the home."

Again I decided to ask him a question. "Who is the governor?" I was not sure what type of answer I would get.

"Titus is the governor." The reply was very quick.

Naphro continued with his account of that lifetime. "I am heading back home to my wife. My workshop is attached to our living area."

He then described his working quarters to me, followed by a description of his wife. "My workshop is on the main floor. My workers are repairing a statue in the main area. A door off to the left leads into the entrance of our living quarters. As soon as I enter, my beautiful wife, Claudia, greets me. She has lovely, long black hair and a great figure. Just like a Greek statue!" A pause.

"Claudia is not too happy right now," exclaimed Naphro.

"Can you tell us why she is not happy?" I asked with curiosity.

His facial expression twisted a bit as he replied. "She and our servants are tired of cleaning up the black soot that comes from the mountain. I explained to her that this is an order from Governor Titus. I tell her we should be proud that we are helping to keep our city streets clean. She does not agree with me."

At this point I ask Naphro to take in a deep breath and move ahead to the next major event in that lifetime. He follows my instructions and appears very relaxed for a brief moment. Then all hell breaks loose!

"The mountain is exploding and the ground is shaking. It's frightening! It is hard to see the sky with all the stones and soot raining down on us. People are screaming and crying. Many of them are in the streets moving toward the shoreline."

"I can see a soldier on a horse trying to calm everyone down. Oh, no. The soldier is falling off the horse onto the street. People are running by him. They are all panicking."

"What are you doing?" I asked Naphro.

"I am on the street not far from the civic center. I am worried about my wife and I must return to my home to be with her. We need to leave Herculaneum as soon as possible. It is terrible here. I must find my wife. I am worried about her."

My client was in a nervous state. He was having a difficult time returning to his home. All the frantic people passing by him, heading toward the shoreline, slowed his passage.

Naphro finally turned around and headed toward the sea. As he told his story, I felt like I was right there watching the scene unfold on a television or movie screen. As he spoke, I watched the scene in my mind of the Roman soldier on a brown horse at a street intersection. The soldier was trying to help people, directing them and giving words of encouragement. His brown horse started to act up, stood up on its back hooves. This action sent the soldier sprawling onto the street as people desperately pushed by him. The maddening scene continued as Naphro rushed toward the sea.

He made it to the shoreline and then took refuge in a boat shelter that resembled a tunnel. It was not far from the water. As he was crowded in there with everyone else, he remarked, "It is too hot. I can't breathe. Oh no. What an awful explosion!" My client's body jerked and twisted. He then settled down with normal breathing patterns. Those were the last moments of that lifetime.

Gently, I guided Tom back from his past-life journey into the present. He slowly opened his eyes, looked at me, and said, "Sorry I fell asleep." He did not remember any of the events of that intense past-life recall. I knew that I should have made suggestions to him to remember or recall his previous lifetime while he was still in that deep, altered state of consciousness.

I thought it was amazing that he had not remembered any of it. During the session he appeared to be in a relaxed state and talked to me steadily. It was like we were having a regular conversation as he lay there vividly detailing all of the events from that previous embodiment.

Neither I nor my client was aware of Roman history at the time of this session. I decided to do some research on Herculaneum and the Roman governor Titus. Sure enough, Titus Flavius, the son of the Emperor Vespasian, was the governor in this area. He had estates in both Herculaneum and nearby Pompeii. In 79 CE, he lived there. Upon the death of Vespasian, Titus was recalled to Rome. He became emperor on June 24 in the year 79. Shortly afterward, in August, Mount Vesuvius erupted and destroyed both Herculaneum and Pompeii.

Upon doing further research, I found out some fascinating things about that time in Herculaneum. The shoreline now is about five hundred meters away from its location back then. It had silted up through the centuries. There were several boat shelters near the former shore that resembled caves. Each shelter had a Roman arch at the entrance. Archaeologists had always surmised that most of the residents of Herculaneum had successfully fled the city and survived the eruption of Mount Vesuvius. When archaeologists did excavations in these boat shelters, however, they found many bodies all huddled together.

These victims came from all walks of life, poor and rich. Gold jewelry and coins were found amongst the victims. So, it appeared that many people had sought shelter there and perished near the early shoreline. Herculaneum was hit by a huge pyroclastic surge of scalding hot lava. The way that Naphro described the events to me was exactly as they had unfolded.

Not all of the ancient Roman town of Herculaneum has been excavated. If they were to excavate more, I am sure they would find the remains of the palace of Vespasian's son Titus, who was the governor up to two months before the time of the ill-fated eruption. This would be a major archaeological discovery. All the artifacts that are there buried below the ground would be exciting to discover.

Tom was a janitor at the time of the session. He loved to clean and get rid of the dirt. He enjoyed it immensely. Perhaps this strange feeling or characteristic came from the fact that he also took intense pride in helping to clean the ash off of the streets of his hometown of Herculaneum in a previous life. This is one example of how some of our characteristics or even our idiosyncrasies can be found to originate in a previous embodiment.

Years later Tom became an Anglican priest and moved ahead with his present life.

Personal Preferences

When I talk about someone's characteristics being brought forward, I also have to include likes and dislikes. Sometimes we do not like a certain type of food or some style of clothing. Or perhaps we have a great dislike for a certain person. This person may be friendly and caring, but we still dislike the individual. Or we have a very strong connection to a person we've just met. It is as if we knew him or her all of our lives. In most cases we do not know why we possess these intense likes and dislikes. All we know is that we have these intense feelings about something or someone.

It is often the eyes that draw us to the individual. We recognize something in the eyes. The eyes are truly the windows to the soul. It is here that a past-life connection can be remembered.

We come back in family groups and repeat similar situations over and over until we get it right. We learn from each of these incarnations. We break our karmic debts and connections to other people. This is all part of the growth of the soul.

We've discussed likes and dislikes. As I mentioned, these dislikes can extend to food or clothing as well. The following story is a great example of this.

Joe came to see me for a regression several years ago. He lay down on the sofa, relaxed, and soon I was able to guide him into a deep, altered state. He was one of those individuals who can be hypnotized very easily.

As the regression unfolded, Joe described a scene that takes place in the wild American West. Although Joe was Canadian, his speech changed in this altered state of consciousness. He described the past-life event with a slow Western drawl.

"I'm hidin' behind a bunch of big rocks near the waterin' hole. Mah horse is nearby. It's hotter 'n hell," he complained. "Ah shore wish Ah could fill up mah canteen. Damn hat! The Indians can spot me with mah big white cowboy hat. Stupid hat." Joe seemed nervous and irritated as he lay there.

He hid behind the rock and pondered what to do. He was trapped.

"Indians are hiding in a rock outcrop not too far away. Ah can't git any water without bein' shot by arrows. I've gotta make a run for my horse."

Then Joe recalled how he made a dash for his horse, leapt on its back, and proceeded to gallop away from the rocks and watering hole. He glanced back over his right shoulder and said, "Oh no. An Indian just appeared from behind a rock. He's shootin' an arrow at me."

Joe described the intense smell of leather, sweat, and dust. He could feel the heat of the soaring sun above. "I can feel the arrow in mah back. I'm slidin' off the horse and onto the dusty ground."

His last comment made about that incarnation was "Stupid hat!"

Obviously, Joe disliked his cowboy hat in that lifetime because it was easy for the Indians to spot him.

When I guided Joe back into a normal state of consciousness, he felt great. He had always had an interest in and fascination with the Old West. This recall made perfect sense to him.

Joe does not like wearing any type of hat. In the business that he owned, many of his employees wore farm or ball caps. Not Joe. He has always disliked wearing a hat ever since he can remember. Obviously, this type of attitude originated from that lifetime as a cowboy.

When you possess a distinct dislike for someone or something but do not know why, perhaps you should explore a few of your previous embodiments on this planet. Answers can be found there.

Healing from Emotional Pain

This next story takes us back to World War II. When a young life is cut short by some tragedy—in this case, a global conflict—the reincarnation cycle of life to death and then rebirth is greatly disturbed.

Dick was a prime example of this situation. He was a young man who worked as a hair stylist. He was intrigued by what I did and decided to have a past-life session with me.

I instructed Dick to relax in the recliner. Using guided meditation, I gently coaxed him into a very deep altered state of consciousness. He was a very good subject and went into the required state very quickly. The story that unfolded was fascinating, but at the same time extremely sad.

"All right, Dick, tell me where you are and what is happening." I leaned back in the chair and waited for the answer.

"I'm in the kitchen of our family farmhouse. I'm very nervous." Dick's face was wrinkled up as he spoke.

"Why are you nervous?" I asked with interest.

"I'm waiting for a letter from the War Department. I'm going into the military as soon as I receive my notice. I expect it any day now. I don't want to go. My parents are aging and I'm their only child. But I know I must do my part." Dick's eyes were moving rapidly under his closed eyelids. He was focused on this scene.

In a few moments, he continued with his tale. "Oh. Here comes the mailman. He has a letter for me. It has the government logo on it. I'm opening it with great reluctance."

"What does the government letter say?" I was curious.

"I'm to report for basic training very soon. I need to go to some place near Chicago. I'm upset about it. I have to tell my parents now."

Dick soon described his conversation with his aging parents. He explained how they all were crying and hugging each other. His dad said he would look after the farm until Dick returned from the war.

The next scene unfolded. Dick was standing in a train station in Chicago. He was waiting for a train to take him to Camp Pendleton in California. This was where his final training would take place. He was going to be an observer in a bomber. He mentioned that his Marine uniform had his name tag on his shirt as Johnson instead of Johansen. There had been a mix-up and that was the name he was given. Dick thought it was no big deal having his name changed to this version.

He could hear the trains going by as he stood there waiting for his own train ride. His hat was neatly tucked upon one shoulder and hung down loosely. During this time, the air force of the United States was not a separate branch of the military; the army and the navy supplied most of the airplanes for the war. The U.S. Marines sometimes worked in conjunction with the army and navy.

Dick then described his stay at Camp Pendleton, a new Marine base opened up because of the war. With great detail he even mentioned one of the meals he ate in the mess hall. He gave the names of the cooks and the fellow soldiers who sat at the dining table with him. He mentioned that the eggs and bacon tasted great. The coffee was a bit strong but he could handle it.

In the next past-life scene, Dick commented on boarding a transport ship that was headed to Hawaii.

Dick talked about the men below deck on the troop ship he was on. A hammock was slung across a space, along with many others. This was where all of the men sat around and talked. Various wooden benches were placed there. Friendly games of poker took place while the ship made its way to Hawaii. A large convoy of ships sailed to this tropical port. My client mentioned a young man named Ben from New Jersey. The two of them were fast becoming friends. All the other fellows were quite friendly.

Finally, the large fleet arrived at its destination. Soon, Dick was stationed in barracks near the airfield where the large bombers were kept. He had already received some training in Camp Pendleton as a navigator's helper. He was busy practicing his newly acquired skills as a navigator's helper for a bomber, possibly a B-29.

The big day arrived finally. Dick reported to the bomber for active duty. Their plane was to go to an airfield on a tropical island not too far from the war front. Once there, they would refuel and then proceed on to their enemy target. He wasn't exactly sure what the target was but suspected that it was an enemy airfield where fighter planes were stationed. At least that was the rumor floating amongst the men on board the bomber. The captain would fill all of them in on the details when they were closer to the objective. There were several other bombers with them that were accompanied by fighter planes. These fighter planes were to provide air support on their mission.

All of the planes arrived at the airfield on a small tropical island. The airstrip had been constructed on the middle of this island. Palm trees and other tropical vegetation surrounded both sides of the small airstrip. There were a few buildings along the right side. A mechanics' shop was one of these small buildings. The other structures were sleeping quarters for the small military staff stationed there. A few American fighter planes sat idle nearby.

After refueling and stretching their legs, the crews of the planes jumped back on board. In moments they were back in the blue tropical skies, heading for their military objective. The flight was uneventful for about an hour, and then total chaos unfolds.

Japanese fighter planes came out of the sky from nowhere. Dick figured they were Zeros, and he described the rising-sun symbol on their wings. Deadly plane fights broke out all around them. He could hear the guns firing and the engines of the planes as they twisted and maneuvered through the busy skies like dozens of bloodthirsty mosquitoes.

There were too many enemy fighter planes. The air support could not handle them all. The American fighter pilots were overwhelmed. Some of them had been hit and were on fire, spinning through the smoke-filled skies. Both sides were suffering from the vicious fighting. Dick noticed a Japanese fighter plane covered in fire plunging to the sea below.

The bomber that Dick was aboard became vulnerable. A few of the Zeros were now free and focused their attack upon the bombers. He could hear the bullets hitting the metal of the plane. More and more lead poured into the bomber, causing considerable damage. Smoke and fire started to fill the cabin area where Dick was sitting in fear. Pain tore into his left arm and his left leg as he was struck by bullets. The plane started to break up. In moments he was swirling amongst twisted metal and wires. It was horrific. He could feel the warm blood flowing over his face, blocking his view of everything. Dick was angry and full of fear. The pain was terrible.

He was extremely upset and said, "I will never see my parents again. Dad will have a hard time looking after the farm. I feel cheated." Anger and sadness was filling him now.

He then moaned, "I feel weak. I think I'm going to pass out." With that Dick became very quiet. He relaxed in the recliner. I watched his breathing going up and down on a normal basis.

It was time to bring him back into this lifetime. Again, I used a special technique to guide him back into the room and fully into his physical body. This involved working with his chakras. I then followed through with more instructions. "When I count to three, feel yourself back in the room and in your body. Feel relaxed and comfortable. One, two, and three. Now, open your eyes."

He opened his eyes, yawned, and then sat up straight. "Wow. Now I know why I can't watch any movies or television shows about World War II. I always felt uncomfortable about this war." His faced showed understanding. Dick had just received a revelation about his feelings toward this time period.

He decided to pass on more information to me as we sat there in my office. "Doug, I have to tell you something. I think it is relevant to this past life." He took a breath and thought carefully about what he would say. "I was born in the United States. I felt pressured to join the armed forces down there. This is something I dreaded. I moved to Canada because I did not want to join the military. I am a pacifist and detest war. It is terrible." Passion was in his eyes.

Dick came to see me a few more times over a period of about a year. Finally, he moved on. I wish him all the best and hope this lifetime is more fruitful now that he has an understanding of how past emotional trauma has influenced this life.

Past-life regression has the ability to heal both emotional and physical pain. In the case of Dick, he was able to heal an emotional pain buried deep within his soul. When we heal the past, we can heal our present and make our future better and brighter. The eternal soul is set free from the bonds of the past. It becomes lighter and less burdened. This allows the soul to grow and move forward. It can embrace a wonderful future.

Health and Pregnancy

The next two case studies or past-life recall stories involve two women who had issues relating to pregnancy. Both of them, through the remembrance of specific past lives, were able to heal the problems that afflicted them in this current lifetime. Both of these clients sought the help of medical experts in order to determine the cause of their problems but to no avail. Here are both of these women's past-life experiences.

Susan was a young, healthy woman who came to see me for a past-life regression. Although she appeared physically healthy, there was a major problem in her life.

Each time she and her husband tried to have a child, they were unsuccessful. Susan would become pregnant and everything would seem fine at first. Then she would have a miscarriage early in the pregnancy. She barely made it into the first trimester, and then mysteriously Susan would lose the fetus.

After four or five attempts at having a child, they both became desperate. Doctors could not find a physiological reason for this situation. Susan decided to try something less conservative. She was at her wit's end when she phoned me and explained her problem. We agreed that past-life therapy was worth a try.

Susan looked nervous and apprehensive when she arrived for her past-life therapy session. Once she sat down in the recliner in my office she started to relax a bit. I instructed her to do some deep-breathing exercises. We talked about the recurring problem for a few moments. Then I felt it was time to begin the session.

"Shut your eyes. Take a deep breath into your lungs and hold it for the count of three. Now, let the breath out slowly." I sipped on my glass of water and then continued. "Take another deep breath in and repeat the process."

Susan was relaxing even more. Her breathing became very regular, much the same as someone sleeping. Now I used guided meditation techniques to get her deeper. In moments, she was in a deep meditative state of consciousness. I could now direct her into a possible past-life recall.

"I want you to tell us what you see. How do you feel here?" I prompted her.

"I'm in a courtyard just in front of my stone and wood house. I feel fine right now. The weather is warm. We live in a small town south of Rome," Susan replied as her eyes moved rapidly below her closed eyelids.

"Let the scene unfold. Describe what you are doing and what is happening around you," I suggested as I focused on her face and her breathing.

"I am pregnant with my first child. It is early yet. I'm just barely showing. I'm so happy about it. My husband is working away from here right now. He should be back in a few days."

Susan went quiet for a minute. Her breathing was regular and relaxed. I sat there quietly, waiting for her story to unfold.

Suddenly, her breathing became quicker and she spoke. "Oh no! The ground is starting to shake violently. I'm falling to the ground. I'm getting up now. It is a terrible earthquake. The high stone walls around me are starting to tumble. I'm very scared."

I advised Susan to let things continue. I knew she needed to experience this in order to get some answers. She needed to heal from this ancient event.

Susan's face was twisted in anguish as she described what was happening, "I'm running past the high stone walls. I must get out into open country. It is much too dangerous here. The walls are starting to fall around me. A stone temple nearby is starting to crumble. By the gods! The whole town is being destroyed. I must get out of here."

She kept talking about the stone walls tumbling down. She also mentioned that several more buildings were falling apart. She was focused on getting into the open, away from the stone.

"I'm trapped! The walls are falling down in front of me. I have to turn around." Susan let out a soft scream. "The stone wall is tumbling down. It's landing on me. I'm lying on the ground with all the heavy stone sitting atop of me. The pain is terrific. My body is being crushed. My unborn child is doomed."

At that moment, I guided Susan out of the body lying in the rubble. I instructed her to float above the scene and tell us what she saw.

"I can see the upper part of my body. I have black hair. I look like I'm dead. I'm wearing a white dress but it is covered in blood. The rest of my body is buried under the stones. Oh, now I can see my angel coming to me. She has her hands out and there is a beautiful smile on her face."

I was pleased about this turn of events. I said, "Let this continue. Let your angel take you to where you need to go. Just allow it to flow."

"She is holding my hand and taking me into an incredible garden. The flowers and the trees are indescribable. This is the most beautiful place I have ever seen. Wow."

Susan kept on relating the scene with her angel. She was now talking to this heavenly messenger, receiving answers that were necessary to her healing and well being. "We are sitting on the grass. My angel is stroking my hair and telling me that I will be healed while I sleep at night. She says I will go to a special healing place where healing angels will work on me. I have nothing to worry about. I will be able to get pregnant and have a child."

Tears were streaking down her face as she related all of these wonderful messages. I let her stay in that realm for a few moments so she could truly enjoy this momentous moment.

Finally, it was time to bring her back into her body and into this room. "All right, Susan, let your guardian angel hug you. She has always been around you and will always be there in the future. Remember how she used to stroke your hair while you slept as a small child. Feel that love and protection."

I continued with the guided meditation and brought her back into the present and into the office. She opened her eyes, smiled, and sat there in deep contemplation for about a minute or two. Susan seemed more at peace. We talked about it and she agreed that she felt much better. In fact, she decided that she would try to get pregnant again. Her attitude was much more positive. There was hope in her young heart.

We said goodbye and I wished her all the best. Later, someone close to me, who knew Susan quite well, passed along the message that Susan had become pregnant and she and her husband did have a child this time. Her whole life had been changed. By hearing such powerful and positive feedback, I felt truly blessed that I had been able to help. I knew that her guardian angel and all her spiritual helpers had helped her. Yes, I believe that the heavenly healers and messengers give us the comfort and support we need in this physical world. They bring us a piece of Heaven and give us hope for our future destiny upon the earth.

Jennifer was also a bright and beautiful young woman who appeared healthy and happy when she came to see me for a past-life therapy session. She sat down in the comfortable recliner, smiled at me nervously, and then said, "My husband and I desperately want to have a child. But I have a couple of issues that are interfering with that goal. First of all, I have an extreme fear of becoming pregnant. I keep thinking that I will die if I have a baby."

Jennifer took a deep breath, composed herself, and then continued, "The second issue involves some type of hormonal imbalance within me. Something is slightly off and seems to be preventing me from getting pregnant. We have tried everything and don't know where to turn."

Jennifer and I talked about this concern for a few moments and then I decided it was time to begin the past-life session. I employed a special energy induction technique to guide her into the right state of consciousness. As stated in chapter 4, the *induction method* is used to allow individuals to enter into an altered state of consciousness in order for them to access past-life information.

She slipped into the proper state very quickly. I sat back in my chair and watched her breathing slow down. She became very relaxed and peaceful. I then guided her in the following manner: "Allow your guardian angel to come to you and give you a big hug. Feel her arms and her beautiful wings surrounding you with light and love. Feel the peace as she holds you here in the garden. Let your arms hug her back and feel love in your heart going out to her. Also, feel the warmth and love that she has for you coming into your chest and whole being."

I was able to watch as a beautiful white light came down from above her head and completely surrounded her as she lay there in a reclined position. Since I possess the ability to see auras and healing colors, this gift allowed me to observe the event in a special way.

Soon her guardian angel was holding her hand and taking her to a special place that Jennifer needed to see. Her angel then let go of her hand. Jennifer started to explore this place and slowly started to describe what she saw. "I'm in a big farmhouse just outside of the city. The home is beautiful and is full of furniture. The furniture looks antique but it appears new."

"Can you tell us what city you live near?" I asked with curiosity.

"I live about a half-hour away from St. Louis. There is a small village close by. My husband and I bought this place in the country so we could get away from the hustle and bustle of a large city. We both love it here."

"All right, in your mind I want you to look down at your body and tell us what you are wearing. Also, can you tell us what the time period is?" I often use this type of probing to allow clients to explore more and receive detailed information. Many clients will answer the time-period question, but not all.

Jennifer's eyes moved back and forth underneath her eyelids. This was a sure sign that she was in a very deep state of altered consciousness. She answered very quietly, "I'm wearing a blue dress and I'm very pregnant." She laughed. "I can barely see my feet because I am so large. Oh, my husband George and I are so happy about having a baby. We can't wait."

"What does your husband do?" I inquired and sipped on my glass of water as I waited for a reply.

"George is a lawyer in the city. He is well known and has lots of clients. He goes to work every morning, then returns home on the train in the evening. He sometimes takes an extra day off on the weekends so we can enjoy our time here together."

Jennifer continued to describe her home and the surrounding garden. She especially enjoyed the huge kitchen with the black-and-white flooring. A newly installed telephone had been placed into the kitchen. She marveled at this wonderful new invention and how it made it easier to talk to George.

After letting my client explore her home and garden in that lifetime, I guided her to move ahead. "Okay. Take a deep breath in and hold it. Now release the breath slowly. As you do, let yourself move ahead to the next major event in that lifetime."

Jennifer followed my instructions easily, and then the next scene from that incarnation unfolded for her. "Oh, no. I am in terrible pain. Something is wrong with the baby. I need help. Our cook is off today and there is no one nearby to help. I have to get to the telephone in the kitchen. I can barely make it. No. The pain is overpowering and I'm collapsing on the black-and-white kitchen floor. I haven't the strength to reach the phone. I'm dizzy and everything is going black in front of my eyes. Warm blood is flowing down my legs and onto the floor. I'm fading fast. Oh, my poor baby. I wish George was here. I'm so scared."

It was at this point, the death scene, that I guided my anxious client to feel her soul slipping out of the body. I instructed her to look down at the traumatic scene below.

Her breathing became less labored and then fell into a gentle rhythm. She spoke slowly, "I can see my body lying on the kitchen floor. There is a lot of blood pooled around my lower extremities. The pain and fear are now gone. I can feel myself floating upward toward a cloud. A beautiful angel is floating toward me with her arms opened up. She is wrapping her arms and wings about me. I can feel all this peace and serenity as she holds me. My angel is taking me to a lovely garden where she is talking to me."

"What is she saying to you?" I asked with a great deal of curiosity.

"Oh. She wants me to analyze that lifetime and understand that I will not have that terrible experience in this lifetime. I can get pregnant and give birth to a healthy baby. She also is telling me that I will have a wonderful, long, and prosperous life if I wish to. I am crying because I'm so happy now. My angel is wiping my tears away. She is sending an incredible amount of love to me. I feel so wonderful.

She tells me it is time to go now, but I can visit her whenever I need to during sleep."

I felt I was being given instructions by her angel, so I guided Jennifer back into this century and into the room. She opened her eyes, smiled at me, and said thank you.

We talked about her previous lifetime for a few moments. She left my office with a sense of peace and happiness.

One day out of the blue, Jennifer phoned me to tell me that she did become pregnant and had a beautiful baby girl. Apparently, according to her doctor, some kind of healing occurred with her hormones and she was able to conceive. She said she and her husband were very happy. We talked for a few moments and said goodbye.

I have not heard from Jennifer since then, but I would like to believe that her life is flowing with love and happiness. It was a great honor and joy to have been part of this wondrous healing process.

As mentioned before, past-life therapy does have the power and ability to heal physical problems. We are multidimensional beings who carry all of our past-life memories and pain within our souls. The lifting of the veil in order to explore a previous incarnation can have wonderful healing properties. Our wounded souls can heal and grow from these experiences.

eight

Children and Past-Life Recall

Train a child in the way he should go, and when
he is old he will not turn from it.

—PROVERBS 22:6

The experiences of children with past-life regression are unique and important to note so that they are not overlooked when they do in fact occur. Children are easier to work with than most adults and enter into altered states of consciousness very quickly. I thought it was best to have a complete chapter on children and past-life recall since the topic is often overlooked. I want to call attention to its occurrence, because there are many benefits for acknowledging children recalling their previous lives.

I have found that children are much more receptive to past-life regression. In most cases, it takes more effort for adults to switch over and use the other area of the brain.

Most kids can relax and let the other side of their brain take over. Their creative, artistic, and imaginative side comes through. Most adults use the analytical part of their brains and are totally focused on the material and physical aspects of this world.

Children are more aware of the heavenly realms and can easily be placed into very receptive states to talk to their angels or vividly recall previous lifetimes. Children use the creative and intuitive side of their brain until about age ten or eleven. At this point, they start to use the logical and analytical side more. In many cases, this has a tendency to shut down their creative, psychic, and spiritual gifts as they focus on living in the modern world. The next story is a great example of a boy who was still able to use those gifts. As is the case throughout this book, all of the names of my clients have been changed.

Resolving Parental Concern

Many years ago a concerned mother telephoned me. She was worried about her ten-year-old son's obsession with mechanics. As I conversed with her, she told me that her son Joe was completely focused on old cars and mechanical magazines. He would tell his mother about living in the city of Calgary. With great detail, Joe described cars from the 1950s and 1960s. He could explain about the motor sizes and horsepower ratings of some of the cars from that era. Even the name and address of a car garage was known by young Joe. Since this boy had never been to this Canadian city in his young lifetime, it perplexed his loving parents.

"My husband and I don't know what to do. We want to bring him to see you. Maybe we can find answers to all of this," Joe's mom told me.

A few days later, the parents showed up with their ten-year-old son. While the parents waited in my living room, I ushered Joe into my office. He slid into the recliner with ease and then stared at me with innocent eyes.

"Okay, Joe, I am going to ask you to close your eyes. Then I want you to start taking slow, relaxing breaths in and release each breath slowly," I instructed my young client.

From that point I guided him into a deeper state of consciousness. In moments, Joe was relaxed enough. His breathing was calm and steady. A composed look was upon his youthful face. Now, it was time to explore his past life.

"Look down at your feet and tell me what you are wearing," I said.

"I'm wearing some type of work shoes. They are all covered in oil stains," he answered quickly.

"Good. Keep looking around and describe what you see. Allow it to flow." I guided Joe and sat back into my armchair.

"I'm in my garage. I can see a couple of cars and I can smell gas and oil. My hands are very dirty." He laughed.

Joe kept talking, and he went into detail about the problem with one of the cars. He knew what was wrong with it but needed to order in a special part in order to fix it properly. The part was expensive, and the owner of the car was balking at paying the money for it. So Joe said he was going to find a way to make do.

"Joe, do you own the garage?" I asked with curiosity.

"No. I'm just the head mechanic. But if I want, I can buy into the shop," he answered.

"Please continue. Tell us more."

"I just love working here. The cars are cool. I've just finished work on my own car. I'm gonna take it out for a spin on the highway soon. I want to see how it performs on an open stretch of road. I can't wait." A smile graced his face as he spoke with excitement.

Joe talked about the great music he listened to as well. The music was all from the 1950s and '60s. He loved the Beatles and some of the other British bands.

That was when I decided to ask him what the date was. "Joe, can you find a calendar in the garage and read the date to me? Look around for a calendar and let me know what you see."

His eyes underneath his closed eyelids moved back and forth, and up and down, as he searched in his mind to find a calendar. "Ah, I found one. I'm in the office looking at it. The date is August 24, 1970."

"All right, I want you to move ahead in that lifetime. Just let the next scene unfold. I also want you to tell us your name if you can." I prompted my young client to move on.

"I'm in my car heading out onto the highway. The car has a lot of power. I wanna see what it will do. My name's Henry, but everyone calls me Hank."

"Can you tell me what type of car you are driving?"

"It's a '68 Mustang. Can't you tell?" My client had a perplexed look on his face as he answered me.

"Yes, of course. I just wanted you to tell me about it. Let the scene unfold." I replied.

"I'm on the highway heading out of the city toward the mountains. I can see them in the distance. The sun is shining, and it's a beautiful fall day here. I'm in the right-hand lane and there's no one around. I've got the road to myself. This is great. I'm gonna open her up." Excitement was evident in his young voice.

As I sat there listening to his conversation, I sensed something was about to happen. As the therapist, I continued listening to his story set in 1970. He needed to let the tale play out for his own sake.

"Wow. The Mustang is flying along the highway. I don't even have the pedal to the floor yet. Here goes nothing! It's going even faster. The speed is great. What a ride."

It was then that Joe's face scrunched up and his breathing sped up rapidly. Now, he was agitated and moved back and forth in the recliner.

"Oh my God, the car is starting to swerve. I'm losing control of it. I'm fighting with the steering wheel but it's no good. No. No. My car is sliding off the highway into a small ravine off to the right. I'm crashing through the brush and grass. My head and my right arm hurts."

My ten-year-old client let out a mild scream as he relayed the event of the accident to me. "The Mustang's flipping over. I'm being tossed about. The pain is terrible. There's blood pouring down my face. It's difficult to see anything. The car has come to a stop. My chest feels terrible. I can't breathe. The pain is horrible. I feel so weak. I feel numb inside and I'm losing consciousness."

Joe's breathing slowed down a second after he finished speaking. His face resumed a more peaceful look.

Now it was time to guide him from this death scene toward something less traumatic. "Feel yourself floating out of the body. Let yourself float above. Feel light as you gaze down upon the scene."

"I can see the remains of my car. It is all twisted and parts of it are strewn down the side of the ravine. There is a white car slowing down and pulling over to the side of the road. I'm floating higher and the scene is disappearing. I can now see white clouds moving around me. It feels like I'm in the middle of a fog. A beautiful angel is coming toward me. She has a smile on her face and her arms are open wide. Her wings are pulled behind her back." My young client had a gentle smile on his face. He looked at peace.

"Just allow it to continue. Enjoy this healing moment. Let your angel talk to you, either verbally or telepathically." I guided him as quietly as I could.

"She is taking me to a beautiful playground and sitting down on a big rock with me. My angel says she loves me very much and I am special. I'm to enjoy this life and follow my heart. If I want to become an engineer, then I should follow this dream. She tells me everything will be all right. Now, she is stroking my hair and smiling at me again. I feel very happy here." Joe was very relaxed as he remained sprawled out in the recliner. His breathing was slow and easy.

I guided Joe back into the room and into this decade. He opened his eyes and smiled at me with a look of happiness. We talked about the past life for a few moments. We also discussed the visit by his guardian angel. He told me that he was able to see angels up to a few months before, but not anymore. Joe hoped he would be able to resume seeing them again.

I said goodbye to Joe and his concerned parents after explaining everything to them. They thought it was a great idea that Joe wanted to become a mechanical engineer. All of them left my home happy. I did not see them after that day. But I hope that everything worked out for this loving family.

The remembrance of that past life as a mechanic may have brought his skills through into this present lifetime. Perhaps, in the future, Joe will become an engineer and make his mark upon this world. One can hope.

Retention of Unique Abilities

This story involves a nine-year-old girl. Her mother loved the work that I did and thought it would be a great idea for her daughter Anna to see me.

Nancy arrived with her daughter one morning for the session. I was introduced to a bright, happy girl who was nearly ten. I noticed pretty, clean colors in her aura as we talked. Both mother and daughter came inside. Nancy made herself comfortable in the living room while Anna and I walked into my office.

I pointed to the recliner, and she immediately made a beeline to it. In moments she was relaxed in the chair. We talked for a few minutes, and I soon discovered that Anna could see the human aura around people. The colors were quite easy for her to see. She thought everyone could do the same thing.

I laughed. "No, not everyone has the ability to see auras. You have a wonderful gift. I hope you keep it for the rest of your life."

After this, we began the session. As a child her mind was still open, and she entered a very deep, altered state of consciousness in mere seconds. Her breathing became very steady and slow. Also, Anna's eyes were moving rapidly beneath her closed eyelids. Again, this was a sign that she was in an alpha state. She was ready for my instructions.

"All right, Anna, I want you to see yourself walking along a path. In your mind, look down at your feet and tell me what you are wearing."

She didn't reply for a few seconds. Her breathing remained steady and her eyes were still moving rapidly beneath the eyelids. When she was ready she started to talk. "My feet are bare. I'm walking on a path in a beautiful forest. I see an opening up ahead. The sun is very bright and there are lots of flowers in this meadow. There are a couple of angels walking toward me. One of them is a woman. She is smiling at me and has her arms open."

"Allow the scene to continue and tell us what you see and how you feel here," I prompted Anna in order to keep the story unfolding.

"My angel is hugging me. She says she is my guardian angel and that she loves me very much. Now, she is taking my hand and walking with me through this pretty area. Up ahead is a stream with grass and rocks. We sit down on the grass and just talk."

I needed to know more. "What is your guardian angel talking to you about?"

"Oh. We're just talking. She says I am very special and she wants me to enjoy my life. I'm supposed to laugh and have lots of fun. When I get older I will find the right type of work that I can do to help many people. Till then she just wants me to just have fun."

Anna kept talking about her angel as they started to play up there in the heavenly fields. She was laughing sometimes as she told me what was happening. A lovely smile was on her face through most of this session.

Finally, Anna moved into a past-life scene where she was a young lady who sold flowers in a small town somewhere in Europe. In this lifetime she was married and was quite happy. She described the small mountains surrounding the town and also detailed its wonderful architecture.

As she continued talking about this previous embodiment, she became sad. My young client spoke with an English accent. Anna was telling me about her young boy dying from a disease. She started to cry as she explained how she and her husband buried their only child. For the remainder of that lifetime, Anna said she was unhappy but survived because of the true love her husband, Mark, had for her. Eventually, I directed Anna ahead to the final moments of that lifetime. "Now, I want you to tell us what you see and how you feel."

With her rough English accent, she exclaimed, "My chest is heavy. I'm having trouble breathing. It hurts. There are a few people sitting around my bed while I lie there. I am very sad. My beloved husband Mark died last year. I miss him so much. I don't want to be here anymore. I wish my angel would come and get me."

Anna's face looked troubled as she lay there in the recliner. She seemed to be straining as she breathed. Then she said, "I feel like I'm floating out of my body. Yes, I can see my guardian angel. She is floating beside me with a smile on her face. She has her hand in mine. Now we are flying through the clouds and going somewhere."

For a few moments, Anna kept breathing in a steady way. Then she continued, "We are going to that meadow where all the pretty flowers are. She is sitting beside the stream and holding my hand. We are just sitting there enjoying the peace and quiet."

"That is great. Just let the scene continue to unfold." I sat back in my chair and listened.

"Now she is telling me that everything will be all right. I will have a wonderful life this time. I will be happy and do great things. I am loved and protected."

These words spoken by Anna were quite comforting to hear. It was time to bring her back to this world. I directed her back into the room in a gentle way.

After the session, I talked with her mother, Nancy. She was quite pleased with the results obtained by her daughter. Both of them left feeling happy.

About two months later, Nancy telephoned me with a serious concern. "Doug, Anna can't see auras anymore. Also, she doesn't see her angels or spirit guides. Everything just closed up about a week or two ago. I don't know what to do. I want her to remain open and use these gifts."

As we talked, I realized what had happened to Anna. Up to about the age of ten, children are still using the creative, artistic side of their brains. After ten, the rational, logical side seems to take over. Children stop using certain areas of the brain such as the pineal gland. This gland actually involves the psychic realm and is important for creativity and other gifts to manifest. When this area of the brain goes unused, these and other gifts die. I explained all of this to Nancy. We decided to do a follow-up session on Anna and see what would happen.

This time when Anna sat in the recliner, I asked her to tell me if she could see the colors around my head. I also wanted to know if she could still see any angels or other celestial beings in the room. "No" was her answer.

I knew I needed to concentrate on her head. I chanted special sounds toward her head as she sat there with her eyes closed. This was followed by energy work that I directed through her body and chakras. A great deal of attention was focused upon the head. After this I asked her, "Anna, look around my head and tell me if you see any colors. Can you see any angels or guides in the room as well?"

Anna opened her eyes and glanced about my head in the crown chakra area for a brief moment. "Yes, I can see blue, green, purple, and some white colors around your head. There is a beautiful angel just floating behind you. She is smiling at me. My head feels like tingles are all over it. I feel really good."

This was great news to hear. Obviously, the chants and energy work had done the job. We were able to reawaken areas of her brain including the pineal gland. At ten, if this gland and other areas of the brain are kept open, there is a very good chance that the child will keep these areas awakened. The individual will use these gifts as adults. Anna was once again using the creative, artistic parts of her brain. I knew she would remain opened and enlightened.

Nancy and Anna left feeling pleased with everything. Anna's mom wanted her daughter to remain open and use her abilities.

A month went by, and then Nancy telephoned again. She said that Anna wanted to see me and had a gift to give me.

When they came into the house, Anna had a great big smile on her young face. She walked up to me and put a piece of paper into my hand. I looked down at the paper. On it were some drawings done with crayons. She pointed at each one of the drawings and explained to me what they were. "This one is my mother. I drew the colors around her body. The one in the middle is my guardian angel. Notice the wings and the colors around her. This other one is a picture of you with your colors around your head. There is your angel right behind you."

Anna was immensely pleased with the drawings. A feeling of warmth filled my heart as I gazed at these artistic creations. My young client obviously had her wonderful gifts working at full steam. It was an honor and blessing to know that I had helped her. This gift of the drawings was worth more than any gold or silver. I considered it priceless. This ten-year-old girl would have a wonderful life and she would laugh and enjoy this world. Moments such as these make it all worthwhile.

I smiled as both Nancy and Anna left. Because of her past-life healing work, I was confident that Anna would be able to retain and use her abilities for the betterment of the world. She and the other special children will help to create a heaven on Earth.

After all, there is hope and opportunity for this earth to raise its vibrations. I believe we will truly have a paradise on Earth in the future, and our work on past lives can only help that process!

Letting Go of Nightmares

Young Joseph was ten years old when his mother brought him to see me. His mother, Jane, was concerned about recurring nightmares that had started to bother her son on a regular basis. About two to three times a week, Joseph would wake up in the middle of the night due to a bad dream, a dream that repeated itself.

Once Joseph settled into a recliner in my office, I asked him about this nightmare. He was a bit uncomfortable as he looked at me and said, "I keep having the same dream. It's really scary."

I then used special guided meditation techniques in order to help Joseph enter into an altered state of consciousness. In a few moments he was relaxed enough. I then guided Joseph to talk about the recurring dream.

He took a few deep breaths and said, "I see myself dressed in a long brown shirt and wearing a pair of boots. I am standing in a forest at nighttime with lots of armed men surrounding me. They grab me and arrest me for something. I think they said I was worshiping the devil and working as a sorcerer or something like that."

He took a deep breath and continued with his story. "I'm innocent. I am not a sorcerer. Someone in the town nearby doesn't like me. He has power and lied to get me in trouble."

"Why would he want to do that to you?" I asked, a bit perplexed.

"I own the land nearby and he wants it. He is jealous. There is a pretty woman who likes me, too. He is interested in her and wants to marry her."

"I see. All right. Please continue with what you see and how you feel." I gently prompted Joseph to continue with the recall of this dream.

"I've been taken to a large public building about two stories high made of wood. I'm standing in a big room with my hands tied behind my back. There are lots of men sitting in front of me in old, wooden chairs. There are people all around watching me."

He continued. "Alex, the man who wants my property, is standing up, pointing his finger at me, and lying about me. He has papers on a table in front of him. He picks up a piece of paper and I can hear him talking." Joseph is looking a bit nervous at this point.

In his dream, Alex is stating, "This is a signed confession from one of the witnesses here today. In this document, the witness states that John Daley, the accused, is a sorcerer and has performed many rituals through the years. I have several other documents by others here who claim the same thing. Many of the witnesses have stated that John Daley performs very strange rituals in the woods at nighttime. They all believe he is a devil worshiper."

Joseph, or John Daley as he was known in that past life, explained further. "Alex and the other men who are judging me brought people to testify against me. It is terrible. All of them are lying. I think some of them have been paid to testify against me, and the rest are very scared. Alex has a lot of power in the town and surrounding area. He associates with very powerful men. Most of them are greedy and unethical."

"Joseph," I said, "I want you to take a deep breath in, hold it, count to three, and then release it. Now, see yourself moving ahead in that lifetime to the next important scene." I sat back in my chair and waited for the next scene to play out.

"No. No. They have found me guilty and condemned me to death. I am to be burnt at the stake as a sorcerer. I can't believe Alex and all of them would do that to me. This is horrible. Armed guards are grabbing my arms and hauling me outside into the main courtyard of the town, near the public square."

Joseph squirmed about in his chair for a moment and then settled down. "There is a stake or a cross in the middle of the courtyard with lots of wood piled up around it. More wood is being added by a few men. I can see armed guards surrounding the edges. Crowds of people are lining up on all sides to watch. I think many of them are scared of Alex and the other powerful men. They are evil and control everything. He is going to steal my land and my girlfriend as well."

The breathing of this ten-year-old became labored as he spoke now. "No. Several armed guards are grabbing me and dragging me up to the wooden stake. They are tying me to it. I'm screaming that I'm innocent, but no one is listening. Now they all step back and two men are taking torches and lighting the kindling. The dry wood is catching fire quickly and starting to come toward me. I can hear and smell the smoke. People are crying and yelling now. The smoke is getting thicker. Oh, no. I can feel the flames starting to burn my legs. The pain is terrible. The heat and the pain are making me pass out.

"The pain is gone. I can see myself floating and looking down at the scene. My body has caught fire and is a torch now. People are just watching in shock. I feel so alone and hurt. As I turn away from the death scene, a beautiful angel with multicolored wings is floating toward me. She has her arms open wide and she is smiling at me. I feel all this love and peace as she is hugging me."

"Let your angel take you to a special healing garden. Let the scene unfold and listen to what she wants to tell you." I made the suggestion to Joseph in a very gentle way.

"We're in a beautiful garden with flowers and trees. It is very peaceful here. She is holding my hand and sitting on the grass in the shade of a huge tree. I feel so relaxed here. My guardian angel, I know that's who she is, is looking at me now and says, 'Joseph, you are special and have wonderful gifts. In this lifetime you will do amazing things and help others. All of your spiritual gifts will awaken fully, allowing you to make a difference in the world. You will never be persecuted in this lifetime for your abilities and beliefs. Enjoy your life. Embrace it and talk to your angels and spirit guides on a regular basis. You will be a teacher and counselor in this lifetime. You will help others to follow their spiritual paths. Know that we love you and will always be with you as you travel your life journey.'

"She is giving me a great big hug and letting me float back down into my body. I know that these beings will always be around me. She says I'm healed and won't have any more of these dreams."

When Joseph opened his eyes a few moments later, he looked at me and smiled. "I feel great," he said.

I talked to Jane, his mother, for a few moments. She was delighted to find out that her son was doing much better. They both looked very happy when they left.

A few months later, I received a call from Jane. She wanted to let me know that Joseph was not having any recurring nightmares anymore. He was happy. Jane said he was now communicating with his angels and spirit guides. According to his mom, Joseph was planning on becoming a teacher when he grew up. I wished them both luck and said goodbye.

Past-life regression therapy is a powerful tool that can be used to heal. Both the human soul and the body can benefit and heal from it. Guidance and wisdom from angels and spirit guides can also be a part of this amazing process. The potential for a wonderful future is the result.

nine

Astral Travel and Past-Life Recall

When you do things from your soul, you feel a
river moving in you, a joy.
　　　—Rumi (1207–73), Persian mystic

The veil between Heaven and Earth has become thinner than it has ever been in our long history. Two events have taken place to allow this to happen. The raising of the Earth's vibrations and the raising of human consciousness are creating wonderful possibilities for many people. These events allow your soul to travel more easily. Your soul can journey to many places and many different levels.

Astral Travel and the Akashic Records

Astral travel and reincarnation are connected. Through astral travel you can explore your previous lifetimes. When you astral travel, you have the ability to leave your body and ascend to the heavenly fields above. Your eternal soul can visit teaching temples, healing gardens, and other wonderful places. One of the places you can visit while in your soul form is the Akashic Records, or Universal Library. Your soul records, which contain all of your previous incarnations, are kept here. You can learn to access these records with special training. This book contains unique techniques to help you visit this amazing repository of universal wisdom. As an experienced past-life therapist, I have used some of these techniques to help my clients visit the Universal Library. When you arrive here in your soul form, you will go to where your soul records are kept and review them.

You might even continue to astral travel and journey to the Universal Library. This special library contains all of your past-life information. If you arrive here, you can open up your soul records and explore many of these previous lifetimes.

Through the years I have noticed that when clients go to the Universal Library, they easily scan their soul records and review or re-live several previous incarnations. I find that clients achieve more success by visiting the Universal Library rather than undergoing a past-life therapy session. Whenever I guide someone into a previous lifetime, the person will see, feel, and experience one or more incarnations. However, when I assist a client to astral travel and guide them to the Universal Library, many of them explore many previous incarnations while in their soul forms. These people access much more information and see more past lives than having a traditional past-life regression.

Astral travel and visiting the Universal Library are great and effective ways to experience many of your previous incarnations in a safe and quick manner. Many clients will either open a book that represents their soul records or experience a vision unfolding before them in the same manner as watching a movie on a screen. This is a powerful way to explore your former incarnations.

When you drift off to sleep, you begin the process of astral travel. This happens on a regular basis. Your eternal soul will slip out of your physical body and travel to amazing places. You as an eternal soul have a valid passport to visit the wonders of Heaven. (There is no paperwork in getting this type of passport, either!) Even regular visits to the Universal Library will be quite possible. For those of you not familiar with this heavenly library, it is a huge repository of all the records of the planet—and the events, including the memory storage, of your previous incarnations. Your soul records are here waiting for your inspection.

A visit to the Universal Library can be a humbling, profound, and sometimes an unsettling experience. This happens when you astral travel and visit this special library. Not only can you access many of your past lives here, but you can access future lives as well. As you become adept at both astral travel and past-life recall, you will visit this amazing library. You will learn to use your library card and receive incredible amounts of past-life and future-life information by using the techniques within this book. So enjoy this library.

Example of Astral Travel
and Akashic Records Work

We are blessed when someone special walks into our lives. The eyes; the smile upon the face; the actions, words, and mannerisms of this person affect us profoundly for the remainder of our days. Juan was one of these precious people.

When Juan came through the door the first time for an initial session, he filled the room with a peaceful but vibrant energy. I motioned for him to sit down in the recliner that faced directly across from my own armchair. As he sat down and gazed at me, I noticed immediately that something was seriously wrong. Juan's neck was swelled up from a large tumor like a bullfrog in a pond.

As in every other session, I asked him to relax in the recliner. He responded to my voice and directions with amazing speed. Like the drop of a hat, he was gone. In seconds, his soul slipped out of his physical body upward out the top of his head. Juan's true essence shimmered just above. His crown chakra surrounding his head glowed with a golden white light. Juan's brown head of hair glistened as if the sun shone upon it. The gold and white luminance continued to swirl gently about this area. Then this shining energy descended into his physical form and flowed around the body as well.

"All right," I said, settling down into my comfortable chair. "I want you to look around and tell me what you see."

"I am sitting on grass underneath a palm tree. I can see large buildings near me." My client's eyes moved rapidly beneath his closed lids as he spoke.

"I want you to stand up," I guided him with a soft voice.

That is exactly what Juan did! He stood up in the room with his eyes shut.

"No. Sit down," I laughed as he sat back down. "*In your mind*, I want you to stand up."

I continued guiding him. "Now, start walking toward these buildings. Describe what you see and how you feel." This time, Juan remained prone in the recliner and did not venture forth on the physical level.

On the spiritual level, it was another story! He was like a kid in a candy shop. With excitement and a big smile on his face, Juan identified these structures and monuments as Egyptian. "I'm inside a temple walking pass the numerous columns. I can smell incense and I can hear the temple singers."

"Who are you and what are you doing here?" I was intrigued with it all.

"I'm a minor priestess. My name is Nefera. Some of the local farmers are worried about the annual flood. They want a blessing from the goddess to ensure that the sacred waters come and flood their lands that sit beside the sacred Nile."

Well, I just had to ask, "Which goddess?"

"Isis. She is the goddess of fertility, but everyone knows that. Why would you even ask me something like that?" A perplexed look was on his face.

"Oh, that's all right. Please continue."

Juan, known as Nefera in that lifetime, resumed speaking. He kept up a running commentary on all that he saw, felt, and knew about that particular past life.

A great deal of information was given freely by this minor priestess. Essentially, it showed the respect given toward the land, the crops, and the spiritual beliefs of that ancient civilization. The earth was loved and cherished. This philosophy is something that our modern world so dearly needs to relearn.

It was time to close the past-life session down and bring Juan back to the present world. "All right, I want you to go to the final moments of your life, Nefara. Tell us what you see and feel. Allow the final scene to unfold."

As expected, Juan, or Nefera, described the death scene, the final moments of that ancient incarnation. "I'm very old. My bones ache. I'm lying in the shade of a beautiful tree. I can feel the warm breeze on my face. My breathing is very labored. Oh, no. There is a great pain in my chest." Juan grabbed his chest as he lay there in the recliner. Then his hands dropped to his side and he became more relaxed. His breathing returned to normal.

Now it was time to bring him back into his body and into the room. "What is happening now? Allow yourself to float above the scene." I watched his face and paid attention to his breathing. During all of this, the beautiful colors still surrounded his body and swirled within his aura. In just a few seconds I was planning on directing Juan back into this physical realm.

Juan and his spiritual helpers had other plans. "I can see beautiful angels coming toward me. One of them is floating right in front of me. Oh, the lights are indescribable. She is smiling at me. She's grabbing my hand and taking me somewhere." The light that covered Juan's head glowed even brighter. A subtle white energy covered his face. A single tear trickled down his cheek.

Well, plans do go awry. I guess I wasn't going to guide him back to Earth right away! Obviously, the powers that be had a greater destination in mind.

With the same amount of passion he had shown during his past-life recall, Juan described his visit to Heaven. He entered a beautiful healing garden in his soul form, escorted by his guardian angel. A few teaching spirit guides were there with him as well.

"I'm floating here." Underneath his closed eyelids, his eyes moved from side to side rapidly. Juan was definitely seeing things. "Several angels—I think they are healing angels—are surrounding me. A couple of the spirit guides are healers, too. I feel as if I'm on a table. All of them are laying their hands on me and sending energy into my body."

My client was very quiet for several minutes. I knew it was best to let things be and not interfere with this angelic healing event. There is a divine wisdom, a universal intelligence, that exists in the heavenly fields. And, yes, it also is present within the earthly realm.

From there, Juan described getting up from the table, walking along a pathway, and then entering a huge library where he saw an old book on a wooden table. "I'm touching the old book. It smells musty."

"These are your soul records. Whenever you want to, you can go to the Universal Library and access your soul records. You can see many past lives when you open the book and look at the pages. Let your soul visit this place as often as you wish," I explained.

Juan was quiet for a moment and then spoke softly, "I'm opening up my soul records and turning the pages. I just stopped at one particular page. I can see glimpses of another lifetime in Egypt when I was a supervisor or overseer of farm lands. I am an expert when it comes to planting wheat and other grains in an optimum manner. I teach farmers how to do all this, and I also look after storage of the grains. I have a beautiful home with lush lands around. My life is wonderful and I feel blessed."

My client then described the final years of that second ancient Egyptian lifetime. He talked about feeling many aches and pains in his body. He then mentioned how he lay down on a bed in his small estate. Sandalwood incense burned profusely as two priests chanted a special song in the room. Juan said that his wife and grown children surrounded his deathbed. Then he mentioned floating above the scene, going through the roof, where he looked down at the estate and lush land that was beside the Nile. From this point he described how his angels and spirit guides started to gather around his soul form.

When everyone up there, including Juan, felt the healing session and visit to the Universal Library were done, he spoke, "The angels and guides are finished. I am being told it is time to return back to Earth."

Well! I had my instructions from above, so I gently guided Juan back into his corporeal body. The colors about him returned to normal as his soul descended down through the crown chakra at the top of his head. His eternal soul slipped into his body like a mist floating through the trees.

He opened his eyes, smiled at me, and said, "I feel much better. I could feel this cool energy working throughout my body. Wow, I was right there in Egypt and up there in a special healing garden. I could really see the library and feel the book. It was great."

Juan, who had a form of lymphatic cancer, came back a few days later, after having a chemotherapy treatment, for a follow-up session with me. An amazing event had taken place. The swollen lymph nodes in his neck and in his abdomen had decreased dramatically in size. For all practical purposes, this should not have happened, since chemotherapy does not normally work in that manner nor does it work that quickly. In any case, it was great to see this wonderful result.

This time we focused on an energy healing session and a past life regression. As before, the beautiful healing colors that came down from the heavenly fields above entered his aura and swirled about his physical body. This all happened as the crown chakra at the top of his head expanded and allowed this Divine Energy to enter into the physical as healing colors.

I felt honored and blessed to be able to watch this happen, to see this amazing light show before my eyes. Through it all, I observed the different hues of light and energy work through his aura, his chakras, his lymphatic system, and into his glands and organs within. As a medical intuitive able to see these colors, it was an amazing event to watch.

Juan was able to handle chemotherapy treatments and to heal himself. He, along with a little help from his spiritual friends above, conquered his disease.

Juan came to see us over a period of four or five years. He received numerous treatments from both my wife and me. Juan continued to recall detailed and interesting past lives through each past-life therapy session he had with me. His strong connection to ancient Egypt and other civilizations allowed him access to the knowledge and the wisdom of the ancients. He brought this valuable information back to the earthly realms, where he used it to help others on this planet.

Meditation and Akashic Records Contemplation Exercise

Along with the techniques and exercises provided in earlier chapters, I thought it would be beneficial to add the following exercise here.

This is a variation of the Past-Life Contemplation exercise found in chapter 5. Again, it is a very easy and relaxing exercise that will allow you to visit the Universal Library and access your soul records. When you do that, you can review or re-live some of your previous incarnations. It is designed for you to employ in your own private and quiet space. A bedroom or a quiet place in your home is the best venue for this exercise.

In the same manner as the Past-Life Contemplation exercise, begin by lighting a few white candles within this private room. Light some incense as well. Sandalwood, frankincense, and myrrh are three of the best ones to use. As mentioned before, smell is a powerful tool that can be used to recall past-life memories and feelings. By using lighted candles and incense in the room, you will also raise the vibrations there, allowing angels and high-minded spirit guides to enter into this area. This protects you while you are in a meditation.

Now, find a comfortable place to sit or lie down. The Chi Deep-Breathing exercise described in chapter 5 should be employed. You do not have to chant May at this time. Simply doing the breathing exercise will be sufficient. Once you have expelled your breath after the third deep-breathing attempt, relax and let your mind drift. As you do this, keep focusing on your breath rising and falling in your chest. Do this for a few moments. Then gaze toward the wall facing you if you are in a sitting position, or gaze at the ceiling above you if you are lying down. Just keep staring through the wall or ceiling and allow your mind to drift. Do not focus on anything in particular.

After a few minutes of this, you are ready for the next phase. Now, say to yourself, "I want to visit the Universal Library. I want to access my soul records." Then let the thought go. At this point you can either leave your eyes open staring at the wall or ceiling, or just close your eyes.

It is crucial that you do the next thing. Let your imagination take over. Imagine that you are floating upward on a cloud toward white marbled buildings. These magnificent buildings should look like the ancient structures found in Rome and Athens. Then imagine that you are floating down onto a stone pathway that leads to one of these Greco-Roman-style buildings made of white marble. Feel an angel or spirit guide beside you as you walk up the ancient white steps and through marble columns, where you stop in front of two huge golden doors. In your mind, ask for your angel or guide to push the great doors open inwards. Then step into the large, spacious ancient library. See the wooden tables, the numerous bookshelves. Imagine that ancient scrolls and old leatherbound books are placed on the tables. See hundreds of books on the many shelves along with pigeonholes filled with papyrus scrolls. Smell the dusty books and ancient scrolls. If you need to, remember walking through a library in this lifetime in order to help you envision this place.

As you do this, there is a very good chance the images in your imagination will switch over to actual visions of a huge library full of many books and scrolls. One moment you will be walking through the golden doors, and the next, you will be exploring this heavenly library and finally you will head to where your soul records are located. Perhaps you will go to a private room where your soul records are placed upon an ancient wooden table. You might even imagine or visualize a spirit guide wearing a long white robe pointing down at an ancient book, your soul records.

In your mind, reach down and open the ancient book containing your soul records. As you turn the yellow pages, a new vision will unfold. Even if you have to imagine a scene, allow it to unfold. Perhaps if you are successful, you will see a past life there as a Roman soldier or a healer working with herbs. As the scenes start to materialize more, you may see buildings and people in strange clothing. You may even smell certain smells, such as flowers or trees or smoke. Remember that the sense of smell can be very strong during a past-life recall. Just drift and let the scenes continue.

Watch the scenes for a few minutes. This previous lifetime may keep unfolding for a bit longer and then finally end, or another previous incarnation may appear on the screen of your mind. If you feel it necessary, turn another page or two in your soul-records book. This action will sometimes allow a new vision of another incarnation to appear. In any event, watch it and study the pictures you are observing.

When you feel you have observed enough, let yourself close the soul-records book and step back. Soon you will be back in the private room attached to the Universal Library. Thank your angels and spirit guides in your thoughts. Then allow your soul to wander back through the ancient library, past the tables and shelves, out the golden doors and down the marble stairs. Sense or see your angel and spirit guide walking side by side. Finally, feel that you are floating on a cloud with both of these loving beings beside you. Let yourself float down into that beautiful garden again. Once you are there in your mind, thank your guardian angel and spirit guide for assisting you. Visualize both these celestial beings as they float slowly away from you.

Now, take another deep breath in and feel yourself back in your private room. Feel the peace and comfort within as you return to normal consciousness.

By using your imagination at the start, you have opened up other areas of your brain. The imagination will change over to an actual astral travel experience where you visit the Universal Library. You can use this variation of the Past-Life Contemplation exercise whenever you wish. The more you practice this exercise, the more times you will visit the Universal Library and access your own soul records. More and more of your past lives will be shown to you. You will become adept at this and even start to receive visions of this special library and also past-life pictures while in a waking state.

You might be on a quiet walk and suddenly a scene of the Akashic Records will flash before your eyes. A scene of a previous embodiment may unfold immediately afterwards. This is an indication that you have lifted the veil that hides the past and revealed one of your incarnations. Use all of the techniques and exercises within this book to enhance your experiences. Allow your eternal soul to journey; healing and understanding will follow.

ten

Dying, Death, and Past-Life Regression

I am confident that there is such a thing as living again, that the living spring from the dead, and that the souls of the dead are in existence.

—SOCRATES

In today's world, there is a crying need for spirituality. With all the worries, fears, and stresses associated with our modern society, there must be a way to find peace and serenity in our everyday existence.

This is equally true for victims of terminal illnesses. There seems to be an explosion of suffering and illness worldwide. Cancer has reached epidemic proportions. Despite all the marvelous advances of medical science, many of us feel lost and helpless in the wake of all this.

How does one cope and make sense of everything today? If one is sick, even terminal, these concerns become greatly compounded. Reality sets in, and fears pervade the mind, causing additional stress and worry. The fear of dying can haunt many people; it can torment a troubled soul.

When one embraces spirituality, these fears and worries are dispelled. Suddenly you look upon life as an amazing journey and know that dying and death are merely the gateways to a better existence. It is a transformation or transition. Rather than fearing death and uncertainty, there is a realization that there is no death.

At the age of nineteen, I had a near-death experience. I was lying in the intensive care unit of a hospital after major bowel surgery. The pain was incredible. One night I experienced my soul leaving my physical body. I floated through the room in my soul form and looked around. I felt free and had no pain at this point. Soon I floated above the hospital and headed toward a tunnel of light. I could see some movement on the other side and wanted to head there—it was beckoning me. Before I could float through the tunnel to the other side, however, two large white beings showed up on both sides of me and prevented me from moving forward. One of these celestial beings said, "It is not your time to go. You must return to Earth and finish your time there."

They gently turned me around and I headed back down, where I went through the ceiling of the hospital and floated back into the dimly lit intensive care unit. I hovered over my sickly body. Reluctantly, I settled back into my physical body. It was then that I felt all the pain return. The male nurse came over and checked on me, then administered a painkiller to me because my heartbeat had sped up. I recovered fully from this experience.

Today, I have no fear of death. I know that something better awaits me on the other side, in Heaven. This experience put me onto my spiritual path and guided me in the work that I now do. It gives me the understanding and compassion to assist others on their paths.

Astral travel, sleep, and death are closely associated with one another: there is little difference between these states. In all of them, your eternal soul or true essence slips out of the physical form and begins to travel about your bedroom, then around your whole home, and finally to higher levels or higher vibrations. These levels are the heavenly fields. Some people who are terminally ill experience this event. They visit Heaven and come back to Earth remembering much of the journey. Many of these individuals are shown previous lifetimes, as you'll see from the stories in this chapter.

Case Studies on Terminal Illness

The following stories or case studies are about my clients. All of them were living with terminal illnesses at the time. Each client was unique and brave through their personal ordeals with their illness. All of them astral traveled as I worked with them, guiding them into the right state of consciousness. As they astral traveled, they also experienced very vivid past-life recalls. Many of them visited the heavenly realms and talked to angels as well. Many people who become deathly ill develop a deep spirituality and open up their psychic abilities, too. I thought it was best to share these case studies with you in order to show that we are truly eternal and there is no death. After all, this is all part of the reincarnation process.

Through the years, I have had many clients, some very healthy, who have visited the Universal Library and experienced previous lifetimes. This special library is available to everyone, not just individuals who are dying.

Often a client will astral travel to higher levels and visit the Universal Library. It is here that they often see several previous lives in a matter of moments as they explore their own soul records. As mentioned, this type of past-life exploration can prove more efficient and much quicker than a traditional past-life recall in which the person sees and feels everything while remaining in their physical body. When the individual in a soul form leaves the body and travels up to Heaven, he or she can experience much more.

In any event, these stories are examples of individuals who had past-life experiences prior to their death in this lifetime that brought them comfort and knowledge that they would live on.

Gracefully Transitioning

Grace came to see me years ago for a session. She had just been diagnosed with breast cancer. Initially, she was angry, scared, and worried.

The first session was an amazing experience for both of us: Grace as the participant and me as the observer. This special lady was a natural energy feeler who relaxed easily and allowed the healing energy from the Creator—Universal Energy, or chi—to flow effortlessly through her body. In no time at all she was able to leave her physical form and astral travel up to the heavenly fields above.

It was a joy and blessing for me to watch the beautiful auric colors descend around her crown chakra, completely covering all of her head. Then these lights moved down through her body, working through the chakras and energy meridians. Light blues, incredible greens, and vibrant whites surrounded her aura as well as filling the entire body. (These were healing colors that can come down from the heavenly fields.) In seconds I watched her face change and saw her guardian angel's face as an overlay staring back at me. Beauty, peace, and serenity shone out.

Through the session, the energy continued in this manner as Grace talked to angels and beings of light. Loved ones who had passed over communicated with her, too. She described a sensation of floating free like a leaf on a gentle wind. Soon she was visiting beautiful gardens and magnificent buildings. Information, knowledge, and wisdom were passed on to her during this wondrous event.

At one point, Grace described walking through two huge golden doors into a vast library. As she gazed around, she saw wooden tables covered with books and scrolls. Countless shelves containing thousands of books and other documents were on both sides of the building along the walls. A bright light streamed down from above, creating an ethereal setting. I asked Grace to continue walking and to tell me what she saw and felt.

"I'm walking through the huge library looking at everything. There are people dressed in strange robes moving about with books and scrolls. I think they are spirit guides.

One of them, a male figure, is floating toward me and wants me to follow him," Grace explained.

"Good. Keep describing what you see and what is happening," I prompted

"The guide is leading me down a long hallway, and at the end of it he opens a wooden door. I follow him into a large room where an old wooden table sits near a window. He points down to an ancient, leather-covered book that is on the table. He tells me it is my soul records and he wants me to look at it." Grace went quiet for a moment. Her eyes underneath the closed lids moved back and forth rapidly, which meant she was in a deep state of altered consciousness.

"Oh! I opened the book containing my soul records and turned to one particular page. The page is turning into a movie. I can see myself then, dressed in a dress from the Old West period. I think I am a dance hall girl. I am young with blond hair and I have a drink in my hand. There is music playing and everyone is laughing. We are all having a great time."

I leaned forward and said, "Take a deep breath in and move to the next scene in that lifetime. Allow it to unfold."

Grace was quiet for a moment and then spoke in an excited manner, "Oh, no. One of my male customers has just walked into the saloon with a gun drawn. He is angry and yelling at me. Tom is his name, I think. He is jealous of my other customers, especially another rival. He is yelling at the top of his lungs. People are ducking for cover. Tom points the gun at me and fires. I can feel a horrible pain in my chest as I fall heavily to the floor. I can't breathe and everything is going dark. I know that I am dying here. I feel sad."

"All right, I want you to float above the scene and watch it for a few moments. Then let your angels and spirit guides come to you," I directed.

"Yes. I'm floating above my body, through the roof and into the sky. A beautiful female angel is putting her hands out to me. She grabs my hand and takes me to a peaceful garden. She tells me to relax here before I continue."

After this, I let Grace go back to her soul records, where she opened another page and saw a different past life unfold. In it she saw herself in a small town in England. This lifetime for her was very peaceful and healing. At the end of that incarnation, she felt herself lie down on a bed and slowly drift out of her body, around the room, and finally up into the sky above. Grace in this lifetime had lived to a very old age. She did notice that many family members were around her when she died. She felt peaceful and fulfilled as she drifted away from that scene.

Finally she went to a beautiful garden and talked to her guardian angel about many things that were personal for her. By the look on her face, she appeared to be enjoying her visit to a garden in the heavenly fields. Her angel was passing on a great deal of information.

It was time to bring her back to Earth. I guided Grace back into the room and her unhealthy body. (It took a bit of work in the form of soothing words and gentle encouragement to bring her back to Earth!) She opened her eyes, and a sparkle was there as she declared, "Wow, that was great! I feel wonderful."

This amazing woman came to see me on a regular basis for her tune-up sessions. She also had regular Reiki sessions with my wife, Carol, during this time.

Grace kept both of us informed as to her physical health, regular family-doctor visits, and appointments with an oncologist. At one point she proudly exclaimed, "I am free of cancer right now. My family doctor thinks I am in remission." Of course, we were all ecstatic about this news.

For the next four or five years, Grace remained relatively healthy, happy, and productive. She was pain-free through most of this period. She was a wonderful mother, wife, and friend to all who were in her life. Grace was known as a great organizer who took care of everyone.

Sadly, her cancer returned. A tumor was found in a lymph node under the right armpit. Her oncologist wanted to operate in order to remove the tumor. Through all of this difficult time she remained strong, positive, and kept her peace of mind—something that was precious to her. Finally, she submitted to the surgical procedure. Unfortunately, within weeks the cancer had spread into her bones. She was fading fast.

With grace and dignity, she organized everything in her remaining days. She asked Carol and me to assist her when it was time for her to leave the confines of this planet and return to her true home in Heaven. (After all, Grace had been visiting Heaven on a regular basis for years.)

A day before she passed over, Carol and I went to visit her in her home at the request of her husband. She was lying in a comatose state with beautiful flowers placed discreetly near her deathbed. I saw a beautiful angel standing by her head, smiling down upon her. Another being of light stood near her feet, touching her legs. With love, both of us touched her hand and quietly said, "It's all right, Grace. You can go home now."

After the funeral, which was treated as a celebration of her full life, and was partially organized by her, Grace's family members came by to visit us. They all stated that Grace's battle with cancer was anything but. Instead, it was a journey! This was the comment she had made several times to everyone.

Grace was fortunate enough to visit the heavenly realm above, experience several previous incarnations, talk to her angels and spirit guides, and communicate with loved ones who had already passed over. She left this earth knowing that there is something better that waits for us after we leave the physical body. She knew she was immortal and that there is no death.

Finding Peace

Karen was a young woman suffering from leukemia. I did not know much about the disease, but I did know that it was very life-threatening. Karen had already had a bone marrow transplant as a form of treatment. Unfortunately, the transplant did not work and she was back to square one.

When Karen came to see me for some energy healing work, she was very sick and pale-skinned; she wore a scarf over her head. All of her hair had been lost due to chemotherapy treatments. She had just completed a round of chemo and was not planning on any more treatments. (At our initial meeting, I was shown a picture of her prior to the onset of her personal pain and suffering. In it, a beautiful woman smiled with black hair that shone with the glow and radiance that only her eternal soul could achieve!)

She was very receptive to the energy. I watched as she became very relaxed and started to drift. I could see beautiful colors starting to descend from above her head, into the crown chakra, and down over the whole body. The colors swirled in similar fashion to the hues found in a rainbow after a summer storm.

Soon, Karen was in a deep receptive state. As the healing colors flowed up, down, and around her body, a wonderful phenomenon began. A white light glowed about her face, and subtly I saw the overlay of her guardian angel gazing back at me. Although Karen had her eyes shut in a deep, altered state of consciousness, intense brown eyes pierced through me. The angelic face had a beaming smile. This ethereal being of light continued to look at me or, rather, through me, during the entire session.

I now felt it was time to guide her into a previous lifetime. Using my voice in a soft and gentle manner, I guided her to a special healing garden in Heaven. "Let yourself relax in this beautiful tropical garden and feel the warmth of the sun on your face. Feel and smell the breeze blowing across your body and your face. Enjoy the fragrance of the flowers, trees, and water. In your mind, look to your right and see your guardian angel and a male spirit guide walking toward you. Watch both of them as they approach along a path through the lovely flowers and shrubs. In front of you, see a multicolored pool of warm water. Also, see, smell, and hear a tropical waterfall splashing onto a rock and into the pool. Feel the intense peace here and know at night-time when you sleep you will visit this special garden up in Heaven. Each time you return from this garden, you will wake up feeling refreshed and healed, knowing that all your gifts and abilities are opening up."

A slight smile appeared on my client's face. Her breathing was deep and slow. I knew she was ready to continue on her spiritual journey and explore a previous lifetime. "Let your angel come to you now and wrap her arms and beautiful white wings around you. Feel the white light and love pouring out of her heart. Feel her soft wings surrounding you. You are both covered now with white and purple light. Enjoy it for a moment. Your guardian angel has always been around you. She used to stroke your hair at night while you slept as a child. She has always been there and will continue to be with you.

"As she releases you, float into the healing pool of water and enjoy the warm, healing water. Immerse yourself completely in this healing pool except for your head. Let the healing water flow around you and heal your soul and body. Then, allow your soul to float underneath the tropical waterfall, which is connected to the healing pool. Feel the multi-colored water descending from the top of your head, down your soul body, and around your feet. It feels like a warm shower as it cleanses your aura, your chakras, and your soul. Now, float out of the waterfall back into the pool of healing water. Let your guardian angel and your spirit guide grab your hands and lift you up into the clouds. See a white light at the end of a tunnel. Move toward the white light with your angel and guide. Step through the light and feel your feet upon the earth."

The overlay of an angelic face continued to gaze at me. Beautiful healing colors still surrounded Karen as she lay there in a very deep state. I watched a slight shimmer of light move up from her prone body, much like looking at heat waves shimmering on a field in the distance in the summertime. She was now astral traveling up into the heavens above.

I asked her quietly, "What do you see on your feet? What type of clothing are you wearing?"

It took about a minute before my client was able to answer. "I'm wearing sandals and I'm walking along a stone pathway. I have a long white robe on, and it feels warm here."

"Great. Tell us what you see and how you feel here."

Karen's breathing was deep and even as she answered, "I feel very peaceful here. There is a gentle breeze blowing my hair back and forth. I can smell water and flowers. As I look around I can see white marble buildings. I think they're Greek. They are magnificent as the sun shines on them. There is a healing temple nearby, enclosed in a beautiful garden. A few women dressed in similar robes are waving and smiling at me. I'm walking toward them and then we all turn and head through the garden into the healing temple. There are some people sitting on marble benches and wooden chairs waiting to see us."

"Can you tell us who you are and what you are doing?" I asked with intense curiosity.

My client's face looked peaceful as she replied, "Yes. I'm a healer. I lay my hands on sick people to help them. I also use different herbal remedies for many of them. I love what I am doing."

I waited for a moment and then prompted her to keep describing what she was doing, "Fine. What is happening now? Describe everything that you see. Let it flow."

"There is a middle-aged lady lying on a table in the middle of the room. White columns surround this room and it is open to the sky above. I can see the blue sky above, along with a few white puffy clouds. The floor is made of stone with benches and seats scattered about the large room. I'm walking forward and putting my hands on the woman's head. She has her eyes closed, and three other female healers are laying their hands on her as well. There is tremendous energy, a warm heat leaving my hands and entering the sick lady's body. I can feel it pulsing and sending healing energy to her as she lies on the healing table.

"The middle-aged woman looks very peaceful as she lies there. Finally, we finish the healing session and take our hands away. I prompt her to sit up, and I explain to her that she needs to come back several more times. I watch her as she gets off the table. She thanks all of us, and then I walk with her toward the door that leads out to the garden. There is an alcove or small room off to the right side. Inside it is a large collection of dried herbs, and some are in leather sacks. I give her some of the herbs and instruct her how to use the medicine. She gives me a silver coin, smiles, and then leaves the healing temple. I feel great that I was able to help her, and I return to the healing room to work on another patient."

It was now time to guide Karen to the next scene, the final scene of that incarnation. "All right, I want you take a deep breath in, hold it, and release it slowly—one, two, and three. Now, I want you to see yourself in the future. Go to the final moments of that lifetime. Allow the scene to unfold and tell us what is happening. Also, let us know how you feel here."

Karen took a few deep breaths in and then continued, "I'm a very old woman now. I'm famous as a great healer here in this part of Greece. People from all over the area come to see me and buy my herbal remedies. I do feel very tired, and my body aches all the time. My hands are a bit swollen, which makes it hard for me to lay them on patients. But I do the best I can."

My young client went quiet for a few seconds and then started talking again. "I don't feel well. My chest hurts and I'm having difficulty breathing. I have to lie down and rest. I'm outside lying on the grass underneath a huge tree. The shade is blocking the heat of the afternoon sun, and there is a nice breeze blowing. Several people, including my fellow healers, friends, and family, are sitting near me or standing above looking down at me. My long hair is blowing, and I can see that it is very gray. My hands feel numb and so do my legs. One of the female healers is holding the upper part of my body up slightly in order to help me breathe more easily. She is using her knees as a support. Oh! I feel a crushing pain in my chest. I can't breathe. Everything is going black."

It was time to guide her out of that lifetime. "Let yourself float above the body and the scene. Feel the pain being released. Ask for your guardian angel and spirit guide to come to you. Feel their comforting presence. Look down at the scene below and tell us what you see."

"I can see my old body lying there on the grass just underneath the huge tree. People are crying and kneeling around my body. One of the healers is stroking my gray hair and looking at my lifeless body. The pain in my chest is completely gone and I can breathe much easier. My guardian angel is holding my right hand, and a male spirit guide is holding my left hand. They are now taking me back to the healing garden in Heaven. We are all floating or flying along. I feel light as a feather. We're back in the garden now."

"Karen, listen to any messages that they want to pass on to you. Let it flow," I suggested as I sat there in the chair.

"Both of them are telling me that I was a healer in that lifetime and that I helped many people. I was at peace within when I died, even though there was some pain for a few moments in my body. They want me to know that the human soul is eternal. I have been here many times before and experienced many events. I will come back again. The next lifetime will be a wonderful experience for me. For now, they want me to feel at peace knowing that I am going back home to Heaven. I have nothing to fear. Although my body may not heal this time, my soul will. I will feel free when I leave this earth."

"My angel and my guide are hugging me. I feel wonderful and at peace. I know they will be around me. Both of them are moving away from me as I stand there."

I guided Karen back into the present and into the room. The beautiful healing colors stayed around Karen as she reclined in the chair for a few seconds. She was covered from the top of her head to her feet in these many different hues of light. As the session ended, her guardian angel's face slowly disappeared and was replaced with the visage of Karen.

Her eyes opened, and she smiled at me and said, "I feel much more at peace." She came back for a few more sessions. Through it all, her humor began to return, and Karen was able to move around more with less discomfort. It was great to see her smile.

But one day it all came to an abrupt end. It was agreed that she would take another stab at a bone marrow transplant. A family member would be the donor.

Shortly after this second attempt at a bone marrow transplant, my wife Carol and I were asked by Karen to come to the hospital to provide some healing energy work. Specifically, it was Carol who would provide a Reiki energy session on this vulnerable young lady.

Of course, this all took place in the isolation section of the local hospital. The caring and helpful nurses instructed us to put on gowns and masks, and to wash our hands using the proper hand-cleaning dispensers.

When we approached the door of the isolation room that Karen was in, a nurse had my wife put on gloves. She also directed Carol to put the mask over her face. And then she entered the room. I stayed back in the hallway nearby. Human nature takes over, and curiosity prods us onward. As Carol worked on her, I glanced in through the glass window. Young Karen's eyes were closed. There was an incredible amount of white light in the room. It surrounded the bed, Carol, and Karen. This light covered her from head to toe. A male angel stood off to the side.

Once my wife had exited the isolation room, I entered it with the mask pulled up over my face. Karen told me about experiencing the past lifetime as a healer in Greece. She mentioned to me that she saw all of this incarnation one night while she lay there in the hospital isolation room. Karen also said that she received glimpses of a few more past lives as well. She felt she needed to see these incarnations in order to make her feel more comfortable. The most important thing was that Karen was at peace within and did not fear a physical death.

After she was discharged, we went to Karen's home at her request. We followed her into her living room, where she lay down on a comfortable sofa. I sat on a chair directly across from her where I could watch everything. We began the session with me guiding her through special deep-breathing techniques. Within seconds, this young woman slipped into a very deep state of consciousness, the same altered state of existence that allows individuals to begin to astral travel. Carol started to do some energy work on her; blue and light green energy flowed from her fingertips. Soon, the healing colors that are associated with the heavenly fields, and exist in our own physical world, started to flow around her. Karen was soon enveloped in this multicolored light. Think of it as a warm and loving embrace from the Creator above.

Suddenly, a mist similar to a light fog began to rise from her prone body. The mist formed the shape of her eternal soul and hovered about four feet above. I stared in awe with tears in my eyes. And then, in a very smooth, fluid motion,

Karen's soul turned over and looked at her physical essence. As the energy session continued with the incredible light show, her immortal soul, a divine spark of the Creator, kept staring down at the physical body.

Finally, when the session ended, her soul floated down, turned upward in the flash of an eye, and settled into the physical form. Karen opened her eyes, smiled, sat up, and said, "I am at peace. Thank you."

That was the last time that we saw her.

This brave young woman faced her own physical mortality. She left this earthly plane a short time later. At least Karen felt the peace in her heart and soul. She knew something better, greater, and infinitely brighter awaited her.

The case studies just shared with you show how powerful the human soul is as it journeys from lifetime to lifetime. The human soul is eternal and linked to God, the Creator, the Great Spirit. A person on a spiritual path knows this and understands that they are a soul with a body and not a body with a soul. The human body is simply the structure that contains the eternal soul while it is here on Earth.

In our modern society most people have an intense fear of death. There is always that fear of the unknown, an uncertainty that contributes to this problem. Through the years, some but not all funeral homes have played upon this fear and the grief of survivors. When someone passes over or rather returns to the heavenly fields above, that person's life should be remembered and celebrated by the loved ones left behind. The soul of that individual is in a much better place.

The trials and tribulations of this earthly world have been left behind.

The process of death is virtually the same as falling asleep, except your soul cannot return to its physical body. After I experienced a near-death incident at the age of nineteen, I changed profoundly. I started to follow a more spiritual path. One thing I do not fear is death. I know for certain that there is something more wonderful waiting for us on the other side.

The recollection of past lives can open up even more doors for you. The knowledge that there is no death, that our souls live forever, gives you a better understanding of who you are and why you are here briefly on this earth.

eleven

Releasing Emotional Pain with Past-Life Regression

*Holding on to anger is like grasping a hot coal
with the intent of throwing it at someone else;
you are the one who gets burned.*
—BUDDHA

When you explore your past lives, it is often to heal an emotional or physical pain. When you access a previous lifetime, the emotions, including anger and hatred, may come to the forefront. They will be very strong, very real. The purpose of remembering the past life is to release the anger, emotional pain, and hatred. Forgiveness is also essential. If you experience a very vivid past-life recall and do not choose to let go of the anger or other negative emotion, then you are defeating the purpose of the regression or recall experience.

So, as part of your spiritual path and growth, it is essential that you learn to release these types of negative emotions.

Forgiveness of people in past lives and people in this lifetime is very important to allow your soul to grow and learn.

Anger and Forgiveness

Prior to returning to Earth, you as a human soul attend a special meeting up in the heavenly fields with special angels and spirit guides. These celestial beings will gather around you and discuss your last incarnation on Earth. You will be shown possible areas that you can be born into for your greatest spiritual growth. All of you will discuss this and then agree upon the right course of action. In essence, you will sign a contract with the heavens above and return to Earth to learn and grow.

When you finally realize that you made a contract with the spiritual beings in Heaven to come back to this planet, the new perspective can make it a bit easier to let this anger from a past incarnation go. (If you are not quite ready to accept this idea or perspective, at least keep an open mind.)

Anger is one of the most dangerous emotions that can reside within all of us. It can destroy lives, relationships, and even countries. It can create wars and suffering. Anger if held within your heart too long can also destroy you.

One of the hardest things for us to do is forgive others. Many of us keep our anger within and hold a grudge for many years. It is important that we forgive the other individual and release that anger within. This allows us to grow emotionally and especially to grow spiritually.

Examples of Releasing Fear for Forgiveness

I have seen the terrible results of someone who holds their anger and resentment toward other people deep inside. These negative emotions become a wound that festers within the soul. Eventually, poisons are released into the body and into the cells. The results are serious health problems. Time and time again I have watched this unfold.

The following case studies will help you to understand the importance of releasing anger and other negative emotions and how past-life regression can assist you in that process if you let it.

Understanding the Source of Anger

Here is one example; I could provide you with several, but this one says it all.

My wife Carol and I knew a lady years ago who managed a few apartment buildings. She was a kind, considerate person who would give you the shirt off her back, as they say.

This generous nature did not extend toward her former husband. Sally had a deep hatred fueled with intense anger and resentment toward him. Whenever she would talk about her ex-husband, her aura would become darker, with angry red colors flowing around her heart area.

I noticed that her heart chakra including both breasts had very dark energy stored there. I knew that Sally would have serious problems in the future if she did not let this hatred go. She needed to forgive her former husband, release the negative emotions, and move on with her life.

We talked to her about this and made suggestions to help her get past this pain. Unfortunately, her mind was made up; she would not forgive nor let it go. Sally was in the middle of court action involving money and real estate that both had shared together. Her spare time was dedicated to pursuing justice in this matter.

"Sally, if you do not let this anger go, it will destroy you. You will die from a disease. I can tell by looking at your heart area that there are some issues starting to manifest there. For your own sake, you must let it go. Move on with your life. Enjoy your life," I warned and advised her with deep concern. I knew she would suffer if she did not heed my advice.

"No. The bastard owes me, and I'm going to get my share. I want my pound of flesh." She was quite emphatic about it. There was no changing her mind.

This lady did decide to try a past-life regression in hopes of finding out about her own past lives. She came to see me and sat down in the recliner. Using special breathing techniques and guided meditation, I was successful in putting Sally into a deep receptive state of consciousness. She was very relaxed and ready to be guided to a previous incarnation with the help of her higher self.

"All right, Sally, I want you to see yourself walking along a path. As you do, look down at your feet and tell me what you see. Are you wearing anything on your feet?" I guided her gently and then sat back in my chair.

"I'm wearing a pair of brown boots and I'm standing on a dirt road. Most of my clothes are brown."

"Good. Now, I want you to describe what you see around you and then describe what you are doing here." I remained relaxed in my seat.

"I'm standing just outside of a wooden building. It has the name of a lawyer on it. Abercrombic, I think. It's warm here and I can see the main street of this small town. A two-story hotel with a wraparound veranda is right beside the law office. Across the dirt street is a saloon. I can even hear the music coming from the place. Horses and buggies are moving up and down the busy street."

"Let the scene continue. Let it flow and describe everything." I sipped on my water and sat back to hear the rest of the story.

"I'm heading inside to talk to the lawyer in the wooden law office. My former partner is there for the meeting as well. I feel very apprehensive and a bit angry. I don't trust him. As soon as I step inside out of the hot sun, I can see him and the lawyer sitting there. They're both looking at me, and Abercrombie is motioning for me to sit down on a wooden chair that is located in front of an antique table. There are paper documents on the table."

"Do you know the name of your former partner? And can you tell us what he looks like?" I asked, suspecting what the answer would be.

"I think his name is Roy Johnson. Oh, I don't believe it. He looks like my ex-husband Tom in this lifetime. His eyes and his voice are the same. We're all sitting in the office now, and the lawyer is opening up one of the documents. He's explaining it to me. I can't believe it. It is a deed for my property, but it's made out to Roy. He says Roy owns the land fair and square. Now he's telling me I have to vacate the premises."

Sally's breathing was speeding up as she spoke. This scene was obviously unsettling to her. I watched her breathing for a few moments and then prompted her to keep going.

"Roy's talking now. He says I owed him a lot of money. That's why he convinced a judge to turn the deed over to him. He's also telling me that he cleared out our mutual bank account for the same reason. The money is now in his own account at a bank in town owned by a friend of his. My former partner has a big smile on his face. I know he is lying through his teeth. I'm so angry. I want to kill him!

"The lawyer is trying to calm me down but I'm too angry. I just punched Roy in his smirking face. He's stepping back from me as I try to put my hands around his lying throat. Abercrombie is pushing my hands back. My breathing is very heavy, very labored. I can feel a pain in my chest starting up. The pain is getting stronger and it's making it hard to breathe. I'm clutching my chest as the pain gets worse. Oh, no. I'm lying on the floor. It feels like an elephant is standing on my chest. My right arm is going numb. I think I'm having a heart attack. Both of them are looking down at me with concern. The lawyer is running out the door for help."

I decided to keep guiding her through this painful event. "Let the scene continue. Describe everything that is happening."

"The pain is horrible. I can't breathe and the room is going dark. I'm losing consciousness. Now I can feel myself floating above the room and the pain is going away. I can see my inert body. I'm a big man in that time with brown hair. There is no movement from my body. Roy is standing beside my body with his arms crossed, looking at me. As I look around I can see a beautiful female angel coming toward me. She has her arms open and she is smiling. I can feel her embracing me. Now my angel is taking me to a garden to sit and talk. She's trying to tell me to let the anger go. She wants me to forgive him and move on with this lifetime.

"I can't do it. I feel betrayed and I'm too angry. I will never forgive the bastard then or now. He stole from me. My angel is holding my hand and stroking my face. Then she says goodbye but will always be nearby whenever I need her. I can see her floating away from me, and she has lovely colors around her. I can feel some peace within."

I felt it was time to bring her back to Earth and the room where the session happened. I guided Sally back into this lifetime and said, "One, two, and three. Feel yourself back in the room and remember everything that you saw. Feel at peace. Now, open your eyes."

It took a few seconds and then Sally opened her eyes and stared at me. We talked about the past-life recall for a few minutes. I encouraged her to forgive her former partner and ex-husband, now and in that previous lifetime. Again, I explained that if she did not forgive him, she would probably make herself sick.

Her last comment to me was "The bastard owes me. I want my money." Sally then got up from the recliner and left. I did not see her after that past-life session. I wondered whatever became of her.

About five years later, I was reading the obituary section of the local newspaper. There she was; her picture and death announcement stared up at me. I was not surprised to find that she had died from breast cancer. Carol and I talked about it. We were a bit saddened about the news. We both knew that she had a choice to make for her greater good. By holding her anger, resentment, and hatred within her heart, she ultimately caused her death.

Now I know that women develop breast cancer for several reasons. Sometimes it is due to genetics. There are many reasons for a woman to become afflicted with this life-threatening disease. One thing I am sure of is that anger can also play a large factor in all of this. In Sally's case, it was the prime reason she became deathly sick.

I truly believe that Sally would not have become sick if she had released the negative emotions that she stored within her heart chakra. If she only chose to forgive her former husband, perhaps she might have survived. The longer pain and anger is stored there, the greater the chance that some serious disorder will develop. The negative emotions will contribute to the release of poisons into the physical body.

Finally Finding Forgiveness

Years ago I knew a very spiritual couple, John and Glenda. Both husband and wife embraced spirituality and explored the fascinating subject of past lives. Both believed strongly in reincarnation. They took several classes from me over a two- or three-year period. Both of them had several past-life regressions with me. Simultaneous past-life recall happened the very first time I guided each of them into a past-life recall.

Initially, when I tried to regress John, a major wall went up. I had to try a few times after counseling him first. Finally, I was successful and John relaxed easily. He entered into a very deep state of altered consciousness. Soon he was ready to explore a previous lifetime, his first attempt at experiencing a past life.

But first I need to share some background information about John. He suffered from a frozen shoulder. Medical doctors could not help him. Whenever my wife did some energy work on John, he would feel relaxed but his frozen shoulder would not move.

It was discovered during his first counseling session with me that his wife had almost left him years ago. She'd had an affair, which affected John very deeply. They worked through this rough road in their marital life and stayed together. Unfortunately, he was not able to release the anger buried within. On some level, he forgave his wife Glenda but he never healed from the anger that he felt.

About the time that John's shoulder froze up permanently, he had a small heart attack. Since he was very stubborn and refused to heal the pain and release the anger, I believed he would eventually experience negative consequences.

Let's return to the initial past-life regression. I guided John into a healing garden up in the heavenly fields. It was there that he met an angel and a male spirit guide. I asked him to focus on both of these celestial beings and let them take him to where he needed to go for his greatest good.

Soon John was describing a scene from World War II. He was in a town near London. I prompted John to tell us what he saw and felt. "I'm walking along a cobblestoned street past quaint-looking buildings about two stories high. The town is very pretty. I'm excited because it is my wedding day. My beloved Grace is going to marry me at the local Anglican church. I have to return to my unit in a few days, so we only have time for a short honeymoon. Oh, well. We will make the best of the situation."

"Can you tell us your name and what the date is?" I asked in hopes of John receiving added information.

My client's eyes moved rapidly back and forth underneath his closed eyelids. Then he spoke quickly, "My name is Andrew. Everyone calls me Andy. It is September 1944, and it looks like we have the Nazis on the run. My unit has to go to Belgium in a few days to fight the Germans. I can't wait to do my duty over there."

"All right, Andy. I want you to move ahead to the very next scene. Describe what you see and how you feel. Allow everything to flow," I suggested mildly to John, or rather Andy, as he was known in that lifetime.

John's breathing was very relaxed as he responded, "I'm inside the church and Grace and I are being married. We have several friends and family there. I feel wonderful. My Grace is a beautiful woman. Wait a minute. I recognize her now as my current wife. Wow, my wife then is my wife now."

My surprised client went quiet for a moment as he analyzed what he had just discovered. It took a few more seconds before he spoke again. "I just slipped the ring on her
finger and I'm kissing her. Everyone is clapping and cheer-
ing. This is great."

John went on to describe their brief honeymoon in
London followed by a tearful goodbye as he then returned
to his military unit. Soon, my client was in Belgium and at
the frontlines fighting the Germans.

"Andy, I want you to describe everything that is happening. Let the scenes unfold." I guided John to discuss the
battle, as I felt this was an important event in that lifetime,
his last one prior to this one.

"I'm not sure, but I think the town is called Bastogne
or something like that. It's early morning and we're in a
forest on a small hill looking down on the occupied town.
One officer is motioning for us to move ahead toward the
town. Artillery has already heavily bombed it. Many of the
buildings have been badly damaged. We're on the edge of
town and several men with me are about to move onto a
street and head toward the center. As I move forward I can
see a few German soldiers pointing their rifles out windows
of damaged buildings. A firefight breaks out, and I shoot
a German who is peering out a second-story window. He
grabs his chest, screams, and falls out the window onto
the street. I can hear the bullets pinging off the buildings
around us. One of my comrades is firing a machine gun
down the street where a bunch of Germans are located.

"I decide to run across the street and make my way
slowly forward. I can feel a terrible pain in my left shoulder.

I fall against a building and collapse inside a doorway. My shoulder hurts like hell, and there's blood running down my arm. I've been shot. Another soldier, I think he's a medic, is running over to me and he starts bandaging up my wound. Then he gives me morphine for the pain. The rest of my unit has moved by down the street and they're cleaning up any remaining resistance. It looks like we are taking the town."

I now had John, or Andy, take in a deep breath, and as he released it, to move ahead to the next event in that lifetime. "I'm lying in a bed in a field hospital. I'm sitting up and my arm is in a sling. I can see a few nurses and doctors moving about the large room. As I glance to my right, a man is coming toward me. I think it's the fellow who passes the mail out to us. He smiles at me and hands me a letter. I thank him and look down at it. It is a letter from my wife, Grace, in England. I'm excited. I can't wait to read it. So, I open it up and start reading. The letter is not what I expected. It's what the Americans call a 'Dear John' letter. Grace is writing that she no longer loves me. She mentions that we rushed into the marriage. We made a mistake. While I've been over here, she rekindled her relationship with an old boyfriend. She wants a divorce and wants to marry him. She claims she is sorry and did not mean to hurt me, but she feels it's best for the both of us. She hopes I find someone else and that I will be happy. I'm so hurt and angry. I would kill her if she was here standing in front of me. I'll never forgive her for what she did to me. She betrayed me. She lied to me."

John, or rather Andy in that lifetime, sobbed quietly for a minute or so. Then the sobbing stopped, and he moved ahead in that lifetime. "I'm an older man. I tried to remarry twice, but both of my marriages ended in divorce. I guess I'm too angry and mean. No one wants to live with me. I still can't forgive Grace for what she did to me in the past. I also drink too much and have liver problems. I'm not very healthy. My doctor says I don't have much time. He and the Anglican priest want me to forgive others from my past and die in peace. I can't do it. I'm still hurt. I will never forgive her. I don't trust women either. They are all the same. They will break your heart and leave you."

It was time to move John to the final moments of that lifetime. He needed closure on this. "Andy, I want you to go to the last moments of that lifetime. Tell us where you are and what is happening. Tell us how you feel also," I directed my client gently but firmly.

John's breathing became labored. "My kidneys are shutting down. My liver is failing and I'm lying in a hospital ward waiting to die. My shoulder stills hurts, and it never worked properly after I was wounded in Belgium. The local priest is nearby, and so is my young son from my second marriage. I can feel myself slipping. The hospital room is going dark. I feel the time is around 1960. I feel like I'm floating out of my body and through the roof. Now I feel free. There is no pain, and I'm soaring through the white clouds. An angel and a male spirit guide are with me. They are taking me back to the garden so we can talk about this lifetime and what I was supposed to learn from it all."

"John, tell us what they are saying. This is important. Please listen to what they say to you." I emphasized the urgency of this meeting.

"My spirit guide is telling me that I need to release the anger and forgive my wife. If I do, my frozen shoulder will heal and I will have a great life. Part of the problem with my shoulder now started back then when I was wounded. I know that they are telling the truth, but I can't forgive her completely. She betrayed me in that lifetime and in this one as well. Now both my angel and my spirit guide are hugging me and saying goodbye. But they will always be nearby."

Now it was time to guide my client back to this incarnation and into the room. I made suggestions for John to remember everything from that previous embodiment. In a few moments he opened his eyes. He looked more peaceful. We talked about that lifetime for a minute or so. Again, I suggested to John that he needed to release the anger and pain and truly forgive his wife. After all, it was important if he was to heal his shoulder and develop a wonderful future life together with his wife.

John thanked me. He even came back a few more times for past-life therapy sessions. These regressions did not dwell upon the forgiveness matter but still helped him with other aspects of his life.

When Glenda, his wife, came to see me for her initial regression, she relaxed easily. She was an easy subject to work with and went very deep in a quick manner. Soon I had her recalling the same lifetime as John, but from a different perspective. She described the same wedding scene in a small town near London. Glenda mentioned that Andy was very forceful and pushed her into the marriage. Upon reflection, she wished she had not given in to his demands and let things be. She knew this would have been better in the long run for the both of them. Glenda, or Grace in that past life, said it was the hardest thing she ever did, writing that letter to Andy.

As the past-life recall continued, Glenda received a powerful insight into that incarnation and the current one. I asked her to explain it to me. "I didn't leave John in this lifetime. I felt extremely guilty. I felt I needed to be responsible and look after him this time. I needed to make up for the last lifetime. I could not hurt him. I love him dearly and I will do what I can to make things right. I have to fix the situation in this lifetime. For some reason we need to be together for the rest of our lives. I guess it is some type of karmic debt I need to break."

When Glenda came back from that past-life recall, we talked about it all. She thought it was incredible that both she and John had remembered the same past life together. My client thought this past-life recall was very important. It made her understand her relationship in a better way.

Glenda did come to see me for a few more past-life therapy sessions. Each time she would go very deep and access incredible amounts of information about past lives. She felt she was much better for doing this.

After the realization of their past lives, John and Glenda came together to work through their anger and find forgiveness.

Forgiveness is the key to healing the heart, the soul, and the body. When you access some of your previous lives, you can use these events to help the healing process. With an open heart full of love, you can achieve so much in this lifetime. This is for your greatest spiritual growth.

When you open up your heart and forgive others, your life will become easier and flow in a more harmonious way. Sometimes exploring a past life will help you to release pain and open up your heart to heal. This allows the true nature of your soul to come forward and help others.

twelve

Making an Appointment with a Past-Life Therapist

The mind is everything; what you think, you become.

—BUDDHA

Many individuals who decide to explore their own past lives will often seek out an experienced past-life therapist. Some people will not know where to turn for help or whom to contact. It is not as easy as picking up the telephone book, going through the yellow pages under "Past-Life Therapist," and then phoning for an appointment. In most situations, it takes a bit of planning, research, and discretion in order to find the right therapist for you.

Where to Look

When seeking out the services of a competent past-life therapist, phone or visit a **metaphysical bookstore**. Most of these specialized bookstores will have information about past-life therapists. Another venue to explore would be any **professional hypnotherapy associations**. Chances are some of the members will be experienced and competent past-life therapists.

The **Internet** is a valuable tool for doing your research. Simply search "past-life therapist" for a certain area. There is a very good chance that you will receive several hits. Then just browse through each one, checking their background and credentials, and contact some of them.

You can also go by **word of mouth** and **referral.** There are various types of people who provide past-life therapy services. Psychics, psychologists, psychiatrists, hypnotists, energy healers, and shamans are some good examples. Many of the people in these various fields are very experienced at this type of work and are very good at it. Ultimately, you have to make the final decision about who you wish to hire.

Through the years, many of my clients and students have explored their previous lifetimes through the services of a psychic or clairvoyant. Of course, a clairvoyant sees "beyond" and receives visions of a paranormal nature, including past lives. If you wish to attempt this approach, feel free to do so. There are many gifted psychics out there. Some of them, including the clairvoyant type, will tune in to your vibrations, as they say, and start to see and sense one of your previous incarnations. You may feel that the psychic or clairvoyant is "right on the mark" as they describe in detail your previous lifetime. Something inside you may resonate with all that is being told to you.

This is fine; this is the start to your past-life exploration.

When you receive past-life information from a psychic and feel good about it all, then it is probably valid. Enjoy the event and let your mind ponder what you have been told.

Now, when you seek out a competent past-life therapist and have an incredible session, you will find this even more effective. In this case, you will see, sense, or feel the emotions from that previous lifetime. It may seem very real to you at the time. You may glean incredible answers and information from this past life therapy session. In the long run, this is much more valid than someone telling you something about a previous lifetime. You get to explore and touch this past-life event in your mind. It can be very profound and helpful to you.

Whether you seek out the services of a psychic or a past-life regressionist, be cautious. Check out the reputation of the prospective psychic or therapist. Talk to people who have had readings or sessions with them. This pertains to regressionists as well, not only psychics or any other category.

Some past-life therapists are trained as psychologists or psychiatrists, but not all. Some therapists are very gifted and experienced at their work without having all the formal education behind them. Just follow your own inner guidance when you seek out a therapist.

Initial Inquiry

When you telephone the individual who provides readings, ask pertinent questions. How much does he or she charge for the reading? How do they receive the information that is being given to you? As you ask your questions, let your own intuitive abilities come forward. Go with what you feel. Do you feel comfortable with the answers you are receiving? And do you feel comfortable with the person you are talking to on the phone? If so, then explore and enjoy this option for your past-life research.

Also, when setting up an appointment to see an experienced therapist, ask for a reference or two. Most therapists who are ethical will have no problem with providing a name or two for you to contact. In many cases, the reputation of the therapist will be all that is needed. Once you are comfortable with the past-life therapist, then proceed on your past-life journey.

Fees

Prices for past-life therapy sessions vary depending on where you live and who you are seeing. Remember that the more qualified and experienced the past-life therapist or psychic, the more costly the session. Of course, the old adage comes to mind: you get what you pay for. So, be prepared to pay a bit more for past-life therapy services.

My sessions here in Western Canada cost $125 per hour and usually take an hour and a half. The average cost will be anywhere between $100 per hour up to $175 per hour, depending on where you live. For instance, if you live in Los

Angeles, the cost for the regression may be higher than in other centers. Past-life regression is very popular in the Los Angeles area and can be highly competitive. Be prepared to pay these prices if you are serious and are seeking an experienced and competent past-life therapist, be it a psychologist or a psychic.

If the cost for the session seems unusually low, then you might consider looking elsewhere. If the price seems a bit on the high side, chances are this individual is experienced and skilled at this type of service. Find what feels right for you.

Keys to a Successful Session

Of course it is your decision about which approach to take. You can go see a psychic or clairvoyant. Then find an experienced past-life therapist and explore a previous embodiment. Sometimes using both methods will help you lift the veil and allow you to experience one or more past lives.

When you do seek out a competent past-life therapist, **have a reason in mind for exploring your past lives.** It is an important journey that you are taking. If you are curious and wish to explore a past life or two, that is fine. Curiosity is a great way to start.

Many people seek out a past-life therapist because they are interested in knowing why they are in their current relationships. This is one of the main reasons why people want to recall a past life. Many answers can be gained about your relationships now by looking into your past incarnations.

Another reason, a very important reason, people want to explore a past life is because of a health condition or the spiritual journey that they are on. Past-life recall is a great way to follow your spiritual path and allow your soul to grow.

Understand the process. It can be helpful to know what to expect. From the many case studies in this book, you should have a good idea of the process. It may also be helpful to know the method that will be used. Many individuals tell me that they cannot be hypnotized. Lots of people have a difficult time being hypnotized by someone for one important reason: the person being hypnotized is not in control of the situation and the possible circumstances. Some individuals automatically put up a barrier because of this. Hypnotherapy as a method to retrieve past-life information has a 33 percent success rate. In other words, only one out of every three people is successful using hypnotism or hypnotherapy. It all depends on how receptive the individual is to hypnotic suggestions. Of course, there are some people who are excellent subjects and enter into a deep hypnotic trance at the drop of a hat. However, most people are not in that category.

Although guided meditation and hypnotism (hypnotherapy) are very similar in approach, there are some key differences between the two. Most people who use a guided meditation method are more successful at recalling past-life memories and feelings. The success rate in this case is much higher than hypnotism. Usually about a 60 percent success rate is achieved.

What is the reason for this? The answer is very simple. When someone guides you gently into a relaxed alpha state, you feel more relaxed and comfortable. Your barrier is lowered and you allow the voice of the practitioner to guide you into the proper place. Many past-life therapists will have the sound of running water or peaceful music in the background as they guide you quietly with the voice. All of this adds to the ambiance or energy of the room. When you feel at peace, your chance of slipping into a deep, altered state and recalling a past life is greatly enhanced.

When you do find a competent past-life therapist, ask that individual what method he or she uses in the past-life session. If it is a type of guided meditation rather than hypnotherapy, then your chances are better that the session will be effective. Some therapists will use special induction techniques along with the guided meditation. This method is even more effective. An induction method such as the one we use in this book is a great technique that offers a higher success rate. My success rate using this approach is about 85 percent. The Chakra Flow induction technique (see chapter 4) works like a charm for most clients.

Some past-life therapists will use a variation of this type of induction. Some will use special chants or breathing techniques in order to help the client enter into the right state of consciousness.

The key to having a successful past-life regression is to **learn to relax and meditate**. When you become adept at meditating, you open up many possibilities. Past-life scenes start to come into your mind. You may even start hearing your inner voice guiding you. Some of your psychic and spiritual gifts will unfold. Angels and spirit guides will be able to communicate with you as well. You might hear an angel's voice or a spirit guide talking to you in your mind.

They will present visions to you while you sleep or are in an altered state of consciousness. Learn to meditate and let the wonderful possibilities open up to you.

The final tip for having a successful session is to **release your fear**. Fear can block a past-life recall from unfolding. If you show up for your past-life session full of fear and worry about what will happen, the chances are you will interfere with your own session. Your fear of the unknown may put a wall up. You may see nothing when you are guided into a relaxed state. I have found in the past that an individual who is full of fear about experiencing a past life will often sabotage the session. The person undergoing the regression may actually see literally nothing but a huge wall in front of them as they visualize.

So, work on releasing that unfounded fear and look forward to the event. See it as an opportunity to explore and learn from your past.

Releasing fear can be helped with simple preparation. Do your homework by meditating. Read books on reincarnation and get yourself into the right frame of mind. Purchase meditation CDs and listen to them.

If you are a natural energy feeler, you may find that you go into a very deep state of consciousness as your own energy flows through your chakras. This phenomenon can happen on its own when you relax and enter into an alpha state. Your own inner intelligence may allow the energy to flow up and down your body and through all of your chakras. This is great if this happens. This ensures that you will go very deep and receive as well as feel some past-life recall.

Enjoy your exploration into your many past lives. Allow yourself to embrace the past, change your present, and create a wonderful future.

Always remember that you are eternal and part of the heavenly light above. Open up your heart and let your soul expand. Walk this precious Earth, watch the magnificent sunsets, and truly enjoy your life. The remembrance of your past lives will comfort you and let you know that you are special. Let your soul be free to explore your past and create a wondrous future for you. Enjoy your soul journey and know that you have a passport to Heaven.

recommended reading

Kasser, Rodolphe, Marvin Meyer, et al., ed. *The Gospel of Judas*. Washington, D.C.: National Geographic Society, 2006.

Lewis, H. Spencer. *Mansions of the Soul: The Cosmic Connection*, 19th ed. San Jose, CA: AMORC, 1981.

Newton, Michael. *Journey of Souls*. St. Paul, MN: Llewellyn, 1994.

Newton, Michael, ed. *Memories of the Afterlife*. Woodbury, MN: Llewellyn, 2009.

Ward, Kaari, et al., ed. *Jesus and His Times*. Pleasantville, NY: Reader's Digest Association, 1990.

Weiss, Brian. *Many Lives, Many Masters*. New York: Touchstone Publications, 1988.

bibliography

De Long, Douglas. *Ancient Healing Techniques.* Woodbury,
  MN: Llewellyn, 2005.

————. *Ancient Teachings for Beginners.* St. Paul, MN:
  Llewellyn, 2000.

————. "My Journey Into Light." *FATE Magazine.* September 2003, 52–55.

————. "Past-Life Pain." *FATE Magazine.* May 2004,
  72–75.

The Holy Bible, King James Version.

Lewis, H. Spencer. *The Mystical Life of Jesus.* San Jose, CA:
  AMORC, 1937 (reprinted in 1965).

————. *The Secret Doctrines of Jesus*. San Jose, CA: AMORC, 1937 (reprinted in 1965).

Pagels, Elaine. *The Gnostic Gospels*. New York: Vintage Books, 1981.

————. *The Gospel of Judas*. Washington, DC: National Geographic Society, 2006.

Petras, Kathryn, and Ross Petras. *The Whole World Book of Quotations: Wisdom from Women and Men around the Globe throughout the Centuries*. New York: Addison-Wesley, 1995.

Prophet, Elizabeth C. *The Lost Teachings of Jesus: Missing Texts, Karma and Reincarnation*. Gardiner, MT: Summit University Press, 1994.

————. *Reincarnation: The Missing Link in Christianity*. Gardiner, MT: Summit University Press, 1997.

Service, Robert. *The Best of Robert Service*. Toronto: McGraw-Hill Ryerson, 1953.

Sri Ramatherin, ed. *Unto Thee I Grant*, 32nd ed. San Jose, CA: AMORC, 1979.

Visalli, Gayle, et al. ed. *After Jesus: The Triumph of Christianity*. Pleasantville, NY: Readers Digest Association, 1992.

Ward, Kaari et al., ed. *Jesus and His Times*. Pleasantville, NY: Reader's Digest Association, 1987.

To Write to the Author

If you wish to contact the author or would like more information about this book, please write to the author in care of Llewellyn Worldwide Ltd., and we will forward your request. Both the author and publisher appreciate hearing from you and learning of your enjoyment of this book and how it has helped you. Llewellyn Worldwide Ltd. cannot guarantee that every letter written to the author can be answered, but all will be forwarded. Please write to:

Douglas De Long
℅ Llewellyn Worldwide
2143 Wooddale Drive
Woodbury, MN 55125-2989

Please enclose a self-addressed stamped envelope for reply,
or $1.00 to cover costs. If outside the USA, enclose
an international postal reply coupon.

Ancient Healing Techniques
A Course in Psychic & Spiritual Development
DOUGLAS DE LONG

Learn to use ancient wisdom to become a powerful healing instrument. Thousands of years ago, the high priests of Egypt performed a special rite called a Final Initiation. Many of these secret ceremonies took place at the Great Pyramid, where initiates performed sacred rituals involving breathing, meditating, and chanting. Afterwards, the students were ready to enter the world as healers.

The author of *Ancient Teachings for Beginners*, Douglas De Long, demonstrates how to perform this Final Initiation rite and other methods for advancing one's psychic and healing abilities. These techniques—involving energy healing, chakra work, colors, chanting, and breathing—are designed to help you achieve spiritual, emotional, and physical well-being.

978-0-7387-0650-4, 264 pp., 5 ³⁄₁₆ x 8   **$15.95**

Ancient
Teachings

For Beginners

Learn about Auras, Chakras, Angels & Astral Projection

DOUGLAS DE LONG

Ancient Teachings for Beginners

Learn About Auras, Chakras, Angels & Astral Projection

DOUGLAS DE LONG

Uncover hidden knowledge from the mystery schools of ages past. This book is designed to awaken or enhance your psychic abilities in a very quick and profound manner. Rather than taking years to achieve this state, you will notice results within a few short weeks, if not instantly. Explore hidden secrets of the ancient mystery schools as you progress through each chapter, from opening your third eye and crown chakras to seeing and reading the human aura.

In addition, you will explore kundalini and chakra arousal techniques that are essential training for aura readers and future medical intuitives. Learn to work safely with spirit guides and angels, practice astral projection, and perform past-life recall.

978-1-56718-214-9, 264 pp., 5 ³⁄₁₆ x 8   **$13.95**

MICHAEL NEWTON, PH.D.

JOURNEY
OF
SOULS

CASE STUDIES OF
LIFE BETWEEN LIVES

Journey of Souls
Case Studies of Life Between Lives
MICHAEL NEWTON, PH.D.

This remarkable book uncovers—for the first time—the mystery of life in the spirit world after death on Earth. Dr. Michael Newton, a hypnotherapist in private practice, has developed his own hypnosis technique to reach his subjects' hidden memories of the hereafter. The narrative is woven as a progressive travelogue around the accounts of twenty-nine people who were placed in a state of super-consciousness. While in deep hypnosis, these subjects describe what has happened to them between their former reincarnations on Earth. They reveal graphic details about how it feels to die, who meets us right after death, what the spirit world is really like, where we go and what we do as souls, and why we choose to come back in certain bodies.

After reading *Journey of Souls*, you will acquire a better understanding of the immortality of the human soul. Plus, you will meet day-to-day personal challenges with a greater sense of purpose as you begin to understand the reasons behind events in your own life.

978-1-56718-485-3, 288 pp., 6 x 9   **$16.95**

MEMORIES
of the
AFTERLIFE

Life Between Lives
Stories of Personal Transformation

Edited by
MICHAEL
NEWTON, PH.D.
with case studies by members of the
NEWTON INSTITUTE

Practical Guide to Past-Life Memories
Twelve Proven Methods
RICHARD WEBSTER

Past-life memories can provide valuable clues as to why we behave the way we do. They can shed light on our purpose in life, and they can help us heal our current wounds. Now you can recall your past lives on your own, without the aid of a hypnotist.

This book includes only the most successful and beneficial methods used in the author's classes. Since one method does not work for everyone, you can experiment with twelve different straightforward techniques to find the best one for you.

This book also answers many questions, such as "Do I have a soul mate?", "Does everyone have a past life?", "Is it dangerous?", and "What about déjà vu?"

978-0-7387-0077-9, 264 pp., 5 ³/₁₆ x 8   **$13.95**

Memories of the Afterlife
Life Between Lives Stories of Personal Transformation
MICHAEL NEWTON, PH.D.

Dr. Michael Newton, best-selling author of *Journey of Souls* and *Destiny of Souls*, returns as the editor and analyst of a series of amazing case studies that highlight the profound impact of spiritual regression on people's everyday lives.

These fascinating true accounts are handpicked and presented by Life Between Lives hypnotherapists certified by the Newton Institute. They feature case studies of real people embarking on life-changing spiritual journeys after recalling their memories of the afterlife: reuniting with soul mates and personal spirit guides, and discovering the ramifications of life and body choices, love relationships, and dreams by communing with their immortal souls. As gems of self-knowledge are revealed, dramatic epiphanies result, enabling these ordinary people to understand adversity in their lives, find emotional healing, realize their true purpose, and forever enrich their lives with new meaning.

978-0-7387-1527-8, 336 pp., 6 x 9 $17.95

Practical Guide to

PAST-LIFE
MEMORIES

Twelve Proven Methods

RICHARD WEBSTER